NO Forbidden FRUIT NO Angry GOD

A DIFFERENT LOOK AT THE STORIES from Adam and Eve to Moses

NO ~~Forbidden~~ FRUIT
NO ~~Angry~~ GOD

A DIFFERENT LOOK AT THE STORIES
~~from~~ Adam and Eve to Moses

DANIEL H. RONIS
and
DONNA SOMERVILLE

BIG MOOSE
PUBLISHING

ISBN: 978-1-989840-78-8 (sc)
ISBN: 978-1-989840-79-5(e)
Big Moose Publishing 11/24

DEDICATION

*To the Matriarchs and Patriarchs and those of faith
who have showed the way*

and

*to those of us who are brave enough to question what we know,
to see what else we can learn.*

CONTENTS

PROLOGUE

by Dan Ronis

This book is a commentary (Midrash) on the people and events in the Five Books of Moses, from Adam and Eve to Moses. The traditional religious and academic commentaries on this subject have delved exhaustively into the stories and their details over centuries of effort. But no definitive conclusions have been reached as to the validity of many of the stories. The thoughts about these stories ranges from complete disbelief, to doubt, to complete acceptance as written.

Since there is little or no outside the Bible information to shed light on these stories, I chose a channelling approach to see if I could get different answers that might be more satisfactory. Information via channelling might be a stretch for many, so for those, please consider these as alternative versions of the

Bible stories. If you focus on the content of the stories rather than the origin, they may well stimulate your thinking and provide new insights regarding the biblical stories and their meaning.

These stories are not just ancient stories with little relevance today. They have had a major cultural impact on societies up to the present day. This is especially true concerning the origin of laws in societies today, how women are treated, and the perception of the role of God in the world which impacts behaviour. If the stories in this book, whatever the origin, cause people to reflect on the traditional stories and their often negative impacts on society then positive changes can begin to occur. I did not begin this book with the idea of changing the conversation regarding the Biblical stories, but that outcome is certainly possible.

This book is neither fiction nor non-fiction. It is an attempt to understand the main biblical stories of the Hebrew Bible (Five Books of Moses) using unofficial sources. On one hand, the Hebrew Bible is one of, if not the most studied book of all time, and yet serious questions about the authenticity of the stories remain unresolved. There is so little other information in existence, historical documents, or archaeological evidence, to prove, disprove or correct the stories. Portions of the stories are so fantastical to the modern brain that many simply do not believe them. Others believe there is some basis in truth, but expend much energy in trying to find a rational explanation; while still others simply accept the stories as written. But what if there was a way to get closer to the real stories, the real happenings? What if there was some basis for all the stories, but they were changed, embellished, mashed together, lost in translation, or written in a way to enhance belief in a Creator?

This book is an attempt to get at the truth, or closer to the truth, if possible, using channelled information derived from a Q&A format. We attempted to answer the following questions: Did the people and events described in the Hebrew Bible actually occur, and if so, what actually happened?

Nicolas de Lange, in his book Atlas of the Jewish World writes, "But the Bible, at least in its older portions, is not a historical record. It sets forth an interpretation of earlier events, a blend of legend, poetry and propaganda, a formative myth of national origins which conceals at least as much as it reveals. We lack the means to test its historical statements, and the actual facts and their chronology are a matter of complex controversy. Archaeology and the records of neighbouring peoples certainly help to fill out the story and to correct or confirm some details, but the picture still remains obscure and fragmentary; some of which may preserve authentic recollection even in their revised form." (de Lange, 1992)[1].

W. Gunther Plaut, in the introduction to his seminal book The Torah, a Modern Commentary writes, "The reader must further understand that the Torah contains a great variety of material: laws, narratives, history, folk tales, songs, proverbial sayings, poetry, and, especially in the early parts of Genesis, myths and legends." In addition, he says, "In this view the various strands of tradition were very old, older than Moses, while others are assignable to him – and were transmitted for many centuries by word of mouth. As the centuries wore in, all of these strands coalesced in popular telling, and in time, probably through the effort of a literary genius of unknown name, they became a single story with many facets. Variants of the same story and even contradictions were left untouched

1   Nicolas de Lange, Atlas of the Jewish World, 1992, page 14

because one did not tamper with sacred documents and also because the ancient era did not demand an either/or, but could say together both sides of the account represented the truth."[2]

Given the statements in the two previous paragraphs, it becomes clear that the Bible has been edited to promote a specific viewpoint to its readers. We assume that the writers and editors had good intentions when they wove oral traditions, stories passed onto generations, prior written records, etc. into one complete text.

The fact that duplicate stories exist attests to the fact that the Bible editors had various sources for each story and in some cases, could not decide if one versus the other story was more authentic and so included both versions. I can just picture the debates, arguments, and passions involved in the discussions by the scribes over what to include or what to reject in writing the final version of the Bible. It must have been interesting times.

In this book we did not try to rewrite the entire Five Books of Moses. We took what we considered were the five most important stories and asked key questions about the people and events of each story. These were the stories of Adam and Eve, Noah and the Flood, Abraham, Joseph, and Moses, which span the Hebrew Bible from Genesis to Deuteronomy. I started each session with a topic (Adam and Eve, for example) and a list of prepared questions.

Donna was not informed in advance of neither the topic nor the questions and so did not know what would be asked

---

2   W. Gunther Plaut, The Torah: A Modern Commentary, 2005, page xxxix

until she was in trance and ready to receive questions. I found it beneficial to start with a general request such as, "Please explain the story of Moses starting with his origin" rather than specific questions at the start. I found that this way I could get a more comprehensive vision of the person and event, and that many subsequent prepared questions were often answered in this initial response.

More importantly, the initial response to a general question immediately generated follow-up questions that were not on my prepared list. It was a balancing act to quickly formulate articulate questions on the spot based on the verbal information just received, while continuing to listen and absorb the on-going response. Once I was satisfied with the new answers, I returned to my prepared questions to continue fleshing out the main points of interest.

Due to the nature of the Q&A approach, the flow of the book is not as smooth as one would expect in a novel or nonfictional text. Due to time constraints, I sometimes did not get to all of my prepared questions (never got to the golden calf), but always got a fascinating, surprising story. I always got far more than I had anticipated.

We believe we have been successful in our efforts to get a different 'view' of the Bible stories. The answers we have obtained show that the events happened, but not always in the ways written about, and that the people were real or were composites of people of a similar nature. We also believe that our stories are more believable, more rational, and more consistent compared to the Bible stories, and as such, are more acceptable to those that wish to believe. We do not present this work as the truth or a truth for many reasons, especially since we mortal humans do not have the capacity to comprehend all the layers of truth in the Universe or an ultimate truth. We can only strive for understanding and knowledge.

THE ART OF CHANNELING

by Donna Somerville

I t was a fascinating experience to review this channeling and add my comments to it. It was the first opportunity I had to sit quietly and become very aware of how I do what I do. It enabled me to realize that I use all my senses in my channel; meaning, I perceive (see), I feel, I know, and I understand.

When I first began as a "reader", I was a seer; meaning that I had visions. I saw what I was to say. I distinctly remember this stage in my development, I became what I would call a translator. I call it translating, because I would see/hear and then describe and put in our language what I was perceiving.

Often in this book, I use the words *sensing* and *feeling*. Then, at other times, the answers are simply spoken as facts, clear and distinct. Sometimes, it is the Counsel that is speaking directly through me. Other times, it is simply facts that I know. I am not involved, although I am paying very close attention and feeling/sensing the energy of the words. This attention to the moment enables me to monitor what is being said and feel the truth of it. This enables me to "know" the Counsel more completely. And when the information is not from the Counsel, my monitoring enables me to feel the clarity and its flow, so that I know the information is not being interfered with from my knowledge or opinions.

It is this attention to the moment, I believe, that enables me to be sure the energy is of a high vibration and is speaking truthfully. At this point in my journey, truth is a feeling to me. And I am always aware of the "feeling of truth" as my marker that this information is clear and not interfered with; that it is here for the highest good of all. The highest good of all is the intention. It is the ground rule in all of my work.

This book has afforded me the opportunity to interact with the Counsel in a way I have not before. That interaction means that at times I was simply their voice; they were speaking through me. When that happened, I could see them, as if I was standing with them and I could hear them speaking, using my voice. There was no dominance of any kind. It was very cooperative. It was a partnership of sorts. And that partnership enabled me to "read" them and that assisted in my perceiving and understanding the true depth of what the Counsel were relaying in the answers.

Way back when, in the beginning of becoming a channel, my fears put very strong restrictions on how the information could come through me. I was very clear that "they", whoever I was channeling at the time, could only use my voice and nothing else. In the beginning, "they" were frightening to me, and so I relied on my restrictions to limit my interaction. Wonderfully, because of free will here on Earth, those restrictions were always obeyed by whatever energies I channeled.

As I grew more comfortable with being a channel, and more trusting of the free will laws, I found that I could allow more interaction with the energy. A teacher suggested that if I let my body move during the channeling, I would become more comfortable in a physical way. At first, I could not. But as I grew in trust, I followed the advice and it proved to be true. Now, I move hands, arms, torso and I am much more comfortable, almost more at one with the energies as they channel through me; much more animated.

In the 1990s, when I started to channel, it was first Guides and Angels, then Archangels like Michael, or Mother Mary. Up until now, my channel has always been used in one-on-one sessions, and so the beings that I channeled were for the benefit of the client I was working with.

I have experimented with councils only once before for a brief period of time in the early 2000s. Working with the Counsel, or other councils for me is an entirely different scope of work and one that I am very grateful to be a part of.

It is also interesting that "the Counsel" was very specific about the spelling of their title. They accepted the "council" title for the first while, but as we moved deeper into the book, they would no longer allow me to let them be called "council". As I came to understand the depth of what the Counsel offered us in this book, I also saw something else. The title they wanted us to use for them was the same word that would describe what the information offered to us is – COUNSEL. The specificness of language is, for me, a huge part of my channeling work and so it is not a surprise to me that they would also be very specific in what their title was to be.

It was also fascinating in those times when the information was simply relayed through me as facts, as knowings, that the Counsel was in the background. I could always feel their interest but could feel that it was not the Counsel speaking. Again, I have experienced such clear and certain knowing in my session work with clients, and so that feeling of knowing was comfortable to me. In this I am not saying that everything we have channeled here is truth. I am saying that it feels as truthful as I can be. I am saying that it feels true as I channeled it; it rings true to me.

THE LANGUAGE OF CHANNELING

Did the Counsel have a language? No, not really. Our connection was more like telepathy. But, when they were speaking through me, it was as if I stood aside and allowed them to use my voice. They did not occupy my physical body, not in the least, but they were allowed to use my voice.

In using my voice, the Counsel has access to my knowledge, my intelligence and my experiences. For me, this is what it means to be a "conscious" channel. There is an interaction between the energies I am channeling and myself. I choose to blend with the energies that I am channeling and so I am one with them. This engages all of my senses. I can perceive (see), feel, know and understand what is coming through me. Then the relaying of what I am sensing is completed using my voice.

THE RIGHT WORD

I am a lover of words, and I find our English language is both limited and amazing at the same time. This limiting amazement has come to me over the years as a channel. As I sense the information, I then attempt to put what I am perceiving, feeling, and understanding into our language. It is through this that I have discovered the limitations of our language. But more importantly, I have discovered that each word we speak has a vibration to it. This idea is driven home here, in our interaction with the Counsel and their insistence upon the use of the "right word".

Often over the years, I have danced with the "right word" because of the vibration that our words have and the images they create. As my channel strengthened, I came to understand that the "right" word contained a specific vibration and image that was to be portrayed. As a result, often in the beginnings of my work as a channel, I would go through several words and would only know I had the "right" word by the feel of the word as it was spoken.

Words are so important and relay not just a meaning, but also share an energy with the listener as well. I can feel when I have chosen the wrong word and until I find the correct word that expresses the correct meaning, I cannot continue in my channel.

In this book, there are places where I use the words *"wrong word"*. When this happens, this is me recognizing in my feeling body that the wrong word has been selected and I must find another before the Counsel will continue. I have to speak the word to know if it is relaying the "right" message and only when the feeling is "right", does the channeled message continue. It is a feeling like the Counsel will not allow me to speak any further, until we have found the "right" word(s) to relay their message.

For a specific example, refer to Section 1, Chapter 6, #2 **Recording 39:45** *How the Counsel Views Earth Event* on page 101. In this example, each time I say a word, "invisible" then "watching", then "participating", I can feel that I have not yet found the "right word" to express what the Counsel is wanting to say.

TIMEFRAME, TIMELINE, TIMELESSNESS

Throughout this book, we are travelling through time to explore these myths. Time is a concept of the Earth plane. As our science has recently discovered, there are other dimensions beyond Earth. In my channeling, I have developed the ability to move through these dimensions. That movement is truly about being trusting and cooperative in the moment.

It has been my experience over the years, that the best way to find the answer is to go to where the answer is. This means going to the timeframe of where the event occurred, and to seek the answer there. In my one-on-one sessions, I use this to move into the childhood of a client and see that childhood with a detached perspective that allows for a clearer understanding of the events.

In the channeling of this book, I used the same method. It is a method I am comfortable with and have developed an instinctive trust with. I believe that the safer I am in my method, the clearer I can be in my work.

There are two words that I use to relay the timing of our answers. The first one is with the word "timeframe". The second one is "timeline". These two words are used in very similar ways. I find that "timeframe" is more structured and specific. When I seek the timeframe, I am seeking to be in the actual moment of the event. I am asking to be moved through time and space to the place that this question can best be answered from. Sometimes I ask to be taken there. Other times I simply move with the Counsel to the memory moment and arrive in the witness of the answer.

When I ask to see the "timeline", this is less structured. Again, I move with the Counsel to the time in question. But with timeline, I get a sense of where this event or person fits into the overview of that period of time. When I perceive timelines, I can see the whole of the timeline, where it is leading, how it is progressing to its end. It is less specific and more a generalized viewpoint of the time in question. They are both words that I use to depict the timing of any event or person we are exploring.

When I ask, *"show me the timeline, please"*, I am asking to see the answer in terms of time as we know it. It means, for me, show me when this happened, show me the unfolding of this event as a timeline. When I do this, I perceive like a door opening and a timeline unfolding in front of me. Then, I follow the timeline to find the answer. An example of this can be found in Section 1, Chapter 1, **#3 Recording 9:14** *Timing of Their Creation* on page 37.

Another discovery I have explored in my channeling is when I move through dimensions and have come to realize that there are spaces of "no time". When I experience this new relationship with time, I call these experiences "timelessness". How I experience this is when I channel and it feels as if I have been channeling for ten minutes, only to have Dan tell me the hour is up. I am surprised, as I have been in this timeless place, and it seems that it has been a very short time to me.

In the channeling of this book, I was able to have another experience of timelessness. I have recognized in the "watching" of the Earth by the Counsel, that they can move seamlessly through time to watch the evolution on the Earth. As I have witnessed this, I realized that the Counsel is beyond time itself, and is not controlled by time as we are on the Earth. I am grateful because in my relationship with the Counsel, I have often moved seamlessly through time with the Counsel as the answers to the questions are presented. For another specific reference to timelessness see Section 1, Chapter 6, #2 **Recording 39:45** *How the Counsel Views Earth Events* on page 101.

THE USE OF THE WORD "THE"

There are several examples where the use of the word "the" precedes the name of a person such as "the Adam", "the Ezra". In these instances, this is how we are using language to distinguish between the person and the potential of that person.

When the word "the" is employed, it is to speak to the consciousness of creation that is taking the form of the person by the same name. There is such a difference between our human self and our consciousness, and I have found that to be one of the most interesting experiences I have had with this book. This distinction is fascinating to me. It truly has shown me the nature of us as humans in a whole new way. The consciousness contained in "the" Adam, and "the" Ezra is the potential of what that human, Adam and Ezra, COULD become. It is their personal choices in living their life that determine what of these potentials are actually achieved. That is our free will in action here on the Earth.

Important in the channelings of this book, this designation of "the" Adam or "the" Ezra is all about the higher wisdoms that are available to each of them as the human they become. When I needed to use the word "the" ahead of a name, the Counsel was being very direct about what higher consciousness they were attempting to insert into the Earth's evolution at that time, and the use of the word "the" was the Counsel's attempt to make this clear.

I find the use of the word "the" a simple way to make a clear distinction between what each of the Counsel's creations have within them as their starting point before EVOLUTION takes over. The Counsel was very wise in using this word, this way. The word "the" was not a choice on my part. Rather, it was a word that I spoke, and my mind paused to question, because in my language this was not the right use of the word. But I have learned over the years to allow the words to be spoken as they need to be spoken. This is a perfect example of what I mean by "right word".

It is a fascinating experience to see our humanity in this way. It puts words to things I have seen in my one-on-one sessions when I have seen the potential in someone, and then I see their limitations to that potential. More often than not, the human is much more limited than their potential is. Our channelings for this book have left me with such hope that we can and will change, simply because we have that potential within us, and EVOLUTION will work with our potential every time. I am truly grateful.

WHERE DID THIS INFORMATION COME FROM?

In my development as a conscious channel, I have worked with various sources of information over the years. These sources that I access are directly related to my beliefs and my trust in the work.

I come from a very religious background of Roman Catholic, and for that I am grateful because it created a relationship with God for me at a very young age. As I have matured and explored my beliefs and relationship with God, my abilities have developed and matured as well. I am still God based, but now I look to an expanded space of God. Now, I work from a place of the Creator of All That Is or Source Potential. I moved from the Roman Catholic God to Source Potential in my search to have a clearer relationship with God, one that did not depend upon religion and dogma.

My ability to allow, and I use that word deliberately, <u>allow</u> myself to channel such energies as are found in this book is something that I have grown into. This book is my second opportunity to work with councils and I have found it very expanding.

The information relayed in this book has come from various sources. For the most part, I took care to name the source of the answers. Sometimes that was not so easy because some of the sources are not as we are. They do not answer to an identity or a name. They will give us a name, because they realize that we understand through identity, and so they cooperate with identity, but it is not part of their makeup.

Identity is a very separated state of being. As I have experienced the dimensions beyond this one, there is far less separation there. There is more unity, more wholeness, more oneness. But, as you will read here, the Counsel is very aware of who we are as humans and how our understanding operates and so they cooperate with it completely.

When I seek to name a source of information, I do so through my senses. I ask to perceive (see), to feel, and to understand the form of being that they are. In the case of the Counsel, I perceive this more as a group of energies. There is separation between each being, but there is also a connection, a union between them that makes it difficult to see each of them as separate. It was as if in my seeking to identify the source of our answers, the Counsel negotiated with me and showed me their union and their separateness at the same time, and then I understood they could be called The Counsel.

In the beginning we used the words "science council", but as my relationship with them grew, I could sense there was so much more to them. I came to truly understand who they were and what their intentions were in their relationship with the Earth and mankind. Once I arrived at this deeper relationship with them, I realized that the science council was a limited title. When I could accept this about them, then it was as if we renegotiated, and "The Counsel" became their new title. This title, the Counsel, feels more flexible, more pliable and much more applicable to them. For with the Counsel, it is not about what, who or where they are. It is about the "counsel" they offer us; the understandings they want to share with us.

But the Counsel is not the only source of our information. By example, in Chapter 4 we explored the time of Abraham, and in this exploration, I found myself in a very different space. I moved away from the Counsel's clear perspective and into another space of what I would call a place of deep faith and reverence.

In an effort for us to truly appreciate and understand the development of faith at the time of Abraham, I was allowed to be present to his prayer space, to sense and experience his relationship to his God. As I experienced this, it was a place of reverence, and of supportive safety. I recognized this as a very sacred and holy space, and the openness I felt within Abraham in his prayer space was amazing. I did recognize the depth of it, because as a child I remember feeling this way about God, myself. In this experience, I realized how faithful men like Abraham were to their God. I experienced their trust and their faith in a very personal way.

But when I compare it to the space I enter into for connection and channel, it is very different. For me now, in my meditations, I connect to Creation. I connect to Creator, but the reverence is gone. There's more equality as I experience the connection to Creator in my channel. In my channel, the reverence is not needed. But my experience of the reverence and supportive safety gave a quality to the information we relayed that enabled me to truly understand and share clearly what Abraham was all about.

And so here is another "source" of our information that I am not really able to give a name or an identity to. It was experiential and that enabled me to feel the fullest extent what the Counsel wanted me to understand. That space of prayer to connect and receive guidance, that humans had in those early days of Abraham, was sacred and complete. I could feel the truth and the faith they had, and that enabled me to understand. I see now that the Counsel needed me to appreciate and understand what they were offering through me to you, so that it would contain a quality of authenticity. It was real to me, and so I am hoping that with the words used to relay it to you in this book, this information can also feel real and authentic to you as well.

And so, it feels now like a good place to explore another source of our information that is offered to you here. This source I have labeled CREATION.

In Section One, Adam and Eve, the Counsel truly opened up and brought me completely into their place of participating in their influence on the Earth. But beyond what the Counsel shared with me, there was again another presence that I could feel that was not the Counsel.

In my experience of what I call CREATION, I became aware of something that was beyond Earth, beyond the Counsel. I was able to call it CREATION, because in my meditations to find a truer relationship with my God, I have reached out into the ethers and explored the raw potential of creation. And when I could feel something drawing me upwards, beyond the Counsel, it was not completely unfamiliar to me.

What was fascinating to me was to feel, or to hold, connection to both the Counsel and CREATION at the same time. I was connected to Counsel and channeling their responses to questions and then I could also sense something else there. It was so cool to realize that CREATION itself was "using" the Counsel, perhaps a better word is "inspiring" the Counsel in its experimental creations on the Earth.

CREATION was a source of information through my experience of it. It felt to me to be curious, as if when the Counsel began creating, CREATION then moved forward to be part of their creations out of its curiosity. It also felt to me to be supportive, understanding and so very encouraging. There was no sense of judgment or rules. It was purely the joy of creating and then witnessing the creations. It felt to be everywhere and not contained in any way, shape or form. It was formless. It was whole. And as a source of information, it was again simply supportive of us knowing, understanding and ultimately creating this book.

HOW DID I DO THIS?

Here I want to explore the tools I used to access this channeled information. It is my hope that those reading this will understand that it is with tools that such a feat is accomplished. I do not believe in "gifts". I believe in faith, dedication to a purpose and a trust of the self in the exploration of what is possible. I believe in EVOLUTION!

It has been a journey to get me to this level of openness and trust. It seems each time I reach a little further, I am then able to reach a little further still. It is not curiosity that drives me. In fact, I believe that curiosity in a channel is a dangerous thing. It is my desire to serve that takes me further and further into my ability. And that is how I fuel my bravery to go further. Do not ever discount how important our bravery is anytime we seek to reach beyond our limits or our comfort zone. Bravery is courage in action and without it, I am not sure who I would be today.

To be specific to the sections and chapters here, let me describe how I came to know Moses in Section Six. I took Moses to be a real person. I sought to know the person who became the story of Moses. I sought to reach the person who inspired the story of Moses and sought to understand him. And, as always, that intent was answered very clearly.

First, I saw Moses. I could describe him to you if you needed me to. I was aware of the details of his robes, his face, his beard, his age. Then, I opened further to him and blended with the person he was in that moment. I could feel what he felt. I explored Moses from the inside out and felt the depth of his faith and his character. I could feel his strengths and his weaknesses. Moses became even more real to me.

Then my senses took me deeper still to truly understand Moses in his role, in his faith and in his life as a man. I felt him in his relationships, in his interactions. I felt the love and respect people around him had for him. My sense of him was then complete. In that place, I could then perceive his conflicts, his determination, and his dedication. Moses had become a complete man to me and from that space I then channeled the information about him.

Was Moses real? The man that I connected with and explored, yes, he was real. Was there ever a real man in history called Moses? Yes, there was a man that CREATION brought me to, and we explored him, and we came to know him. That makes him real to me.

Please notice I have just changed pronoun from "I" to "we". That is <u>very</u> important to me, because I do not do this work on my own. I work with Creator/Creation and ask to be of service through Creation to whatever work I am doing. I become a "we" when I work. That is THE most important thing in my work. My work is never ONLY me. It is ALWAYS "We".

And from this space of WE, we offer this new understanding of old information. Here, we offer an understanding of how we did this. Our hope is that it serves you, that it raises questions in your mind and loosens your hold on what you think you can and cannot do. We hope that it opens your mind to new ideas and exploration through the questions we have raised for you with this book. This book is not offered as new biblical truths, but rather to say what are biblical truths.

As spoken in Chapter Zero, this book, like the Bible, is offered as roadmap to simple understandings; as a method to see our own personal self in terms of who we are becoming. It is offered to make each of us aware that we are still evolving. That EVOLUTION is still at work with us each, individually; to ask if we are in fact cooperating with EVOLUTION or working against it. Are we now driven by what we know and what we want? Or by what is possible and what we can become?

We offer this new perspective of the simple truths that began in Eden, to awaken an idea that they can still have a place in our world today. For these simple truths to be found in our world today, they must first find their way into our individual lives. That can happen when we return to the simplicity of caring for one another's neighbours or family; of supporting one another, friends or foes; of believing in each other through the release of blaming, dominance and "me" first.

It is my fervent hope that we challenge your thinking with the facts as The Counsel has relayed them here, that we touch your heart by making the faith and trust of such men as Abraham and Moses much more real, and that we leave you with food for thought about how CREATION and EVOLUTION do in fact work together and not separately, one against the other.

If I can be this, what else can I be? EVOLUTION. CREATION. Allow them to become more real and see where they can take you, and where they can take our world. Let's continue to evolve and grow. Let go of the feeling of being a finished product and move beyond what we know and what we have become comfortable with. Let this book make you uncomfortable and see what you can find in your discomfort. This is what we did here.

Amen.

Chapter Zero

WHO ACTUALLY WROTE THE BIBLE?

#9 Recording 3:07 *Why Was It Written?*

DR: My question today concerns the Hebrew Bible. There is controversy over its origin. My first question is: what was the intent in writing the Hebrew Bible? Was it written as a spiritual book, or as a document to preserve knowledge, as a history, a moral teaching? Can you explain what the origin of the intent was?

DS: There are several answers to this question. The first answer is that the original writing began because there was a sense that the story telling, from one generation to the next, was weakening. The second reason for the writing was to preserve the story and prevent any further changes – embellishments – to the story itself. The intent was teaching. The intent was **reminding**, and through the reminding, to teach.

There was this process occurring of change and innovation, but they [the elders] did not want the simplistic understandings of the beginnings to be lost. There was peace made with the innovations and changes that were coming, but within it they wanted a foundation of the simple truth upon which all began. And so, the Bible, as you are calling it, the documents and the writings were begun so that the beginnings would not be forgotten.

There was a witness and sense in the older generations that much of the simple could easily be lost in the innovations. We will not say it was lost. But they (the older generations) had witnessed those that did lose their way and hoped that the writings would give them something to find their way back, like a map, when they were lost in the changes and innovations.

It was not meant to be rules. It was meant to be a remembering, because the simplistic beginnings held strength and held root. And there was a fear that the innovations and changes could cause uprooting.

(Note: Throughout the channeled text there will be times when Donna explains further what she is experiencing in channel. These parts will be noted in italics as seen in pages following.)

Up until this point, my awareness of the origins of the writings feels like a knowing, a fact. I am receiving the clear understanding of the why of these writings. At this point, I am describing what I am witnessing as the reasons for the writing the stories of the Bible. I can feel the storyteller's resistance to the responsibility to hold these old truths. I can feel their reverence for those old truths and from that, I feel their desire to write it all down and help preserve the truths in that way. It is an act of reverence as I perceive it.

*Also, I can see and feel the concern of the elder generations. I can feel their acceptance of the innovations, but also their concern of where this is all heading. I can feel their need and hope for these writings. It feels like a loving act to create these writings. **It is not meant as rules or commandments.** It is meant as a loving act of guidance to reverently keep the truth of the beginnings, and have them available, if the innovations lead to a time of losing their (our) way.*

There is something else here. There is a charge around "uprooting". There is a sense of the Counsel's presence, and they wish to say this:

In our witness and our observation of mankind in its evolution, we have often witnessed the destruction of uprootedness. It has been fascinating to see how important the roots are to mankind. It seems the humans are stronger when they have roots. And when they uproot to explore and change, they often get lost in their ways. We appreciated the faith and understanding that arose in the creations of the holy works in writing, because it showed us that the humans themselves were becoming aware of how dangerous uprootedness was.

When the Eden was present, it provided the rootedness. But once the Eden was undone, each was left to find their own rootedness. Many means were developed for the sense of rootedness. Often that was found through your religions, gods, goddesses, and faiths.

We wish to simply confirm that our observations supported the need for anything that could support the feeling of rooted. And as we are using your word rooted, we are meaning that the human knows where they belong, where they can plant themselves and be strong. They know where their sanctuary is, where their home is. It is one of the most interesting evolutionary effects on the humans. They evolved in the way a pack of animals would evolve, hence the tribes and clans. It gave them a sense of belonging and a sense of rootedness. So, this is our witness of the importance of being rooted and the danger of being unrooted, uprooted, to support further the answer to your question.

The Counsel is also allowing the visions of how the packs, the clans, the tribes evolved over generations so that the man you are now can be individualistic in a way that was unknown in the times when the Bible was written.

The individualism of your now time did not exist in the time you are exploring of your Bible. It was what evolved. That is why it is not a sense that the Bible was meant to be commandments or rules, because there was not the individual that needed the commandments or rules. It was to hold what could be forgotten, the simplicity of it. We offer this to you for your consideration and discernment.

#9 Recording 12:20 *About the Storytellers*

DR: How were the oral histories passed on intact from

generation to generation, and how long were they passed on before things were written down?

DS: One tribe could have four families, many, many people, but four family lines, sometimes six. And in each family line there was one designated storyteller. They were taught the stories. It was their job to hold the stories, and it was important that the stories were not embellished. When the storyteller was being trained by the previous storyteller, the stories were rote and told as instructed. Once the storyteller who was training passed away, the new storyteller did sometimes take some embellishments, for what he would think would make the story more interesting. This would be frowned upon greatly by the elders who knew the true story. But there was relief that the storyteller was still telling stories and that the bones of the truth were still strongly there, and unaffected by the embellishments.

Show me the timelines please. Show me the generations of storytellers.

It was the twelfth generation, in some tribes the fifteenth generation, before there was consideration made to the stories becoming something written in some way. We will not say that at the twelfth or fifteenth generation the Bible was written. It was not. But the beginnings of the idea of recording these in another way were discussed. There still was the training of the next generation of storyteller. And so, there was three of four generations where there was oral storytelling and some written storytelling. And then, slowly it transitioned to just the writing.

But the writings still stayed within the family line of the

storyteller. So, the one that was the oral storyteller became the writer of the story. That continued for several generations, and then the education got stronger. There were shifts in education and then each tribe had a scribe. And the scribe would be the one who made sure the stories were written, recorded, and saved.

Interesting, that when the scribes were responsible for the written stories, the stories were not shared as they had been in the oral storytelling time. In the oral storytelling times, the stories were told often, four, five times a month. But once they were written, they were not part of the everyday entertainment of the gathering. There were places they were brought forward, in celebrations, in formal settings, at births, at weddings, at deaths. But they were not part of the everyday life. Once written, that was lost. And then, the stories became the property of the scribes.

When the Bible was written, when the book was put together, it was done by the scribes. And there was discussion about what was the truth in the stories and what were the embellishments. And that is when some of the stories became composites, when they would put more than one story together to come to the one story.

There was no maliciousness. There was no manipulation. It was more that some of the storytellers had added embellishments. And so, the eldest of the family tribe at the time the Bible was being created, would help to uncover from among the embellishments, the original truth. Keeping in mind that embellishments had been added now for eight or ten generations. But simple truth still held and does still hold in those stories. The simple truth is clear. We want to say, "Clear as a bell."

The vision of this movement of the oral storytelling into the written was again, an evolution. I can feel the group of them come together to put the stories into writing. I can feel their dedication to unveiling the "truth" from the embellishments. As I witness all those involved, I can feel their dedication. This is a holy service they are involved in, and each takes it very seriously. Their search for the truth is a holy act.

I can feel the absolute certainty that the guidance in the Bible is as it was meant to be, a map to return to the simple. I can feel how the intent of the writing was, in fact, fulfilled.

DR: Did different families have a person designated to be the recorder, the memorizer of the stories? Did different families then keep different stories, or did they keep all those stories in one mind?

DS: Each storyteller was to be telling the same stories. It was why the training was rote. And it was important to the elder to be sure the younger told the story exactly as it was taught. But as the generations unfolded, as each elder passed away, the younger would then sometimes try to make the story more interesting. But the core of the story as told in each tribe would be the same. There still would be the story of the floods; there still would be the story of the Eden, there still would be the story of Moses, and of Abraham. But the details were where the embellishment made them slightly different.

And so, when the Bible was composed, and we say the word deliberately, when the Bible was composed, the scribes from all these families came together with what their writing said was the story. And then they used the eldest among them to try and sift through the embellishments and come to the truth, the core, of the one story.

#9 Recording 20:13 *The Final Compilation of the Stories*

DR: Was there a well-known man named Ezra who was involved in the final compilation of the Bible stories?

DS: *Show me the time of the compilations. Show me now, please.*

The compilation of what you are calling your Bible was over several generations. We do see the presence of Ezra in the first meetings. He was one of the elders that helped screen through the embellishments. And it was his role until the end of his life. But we will not say that the book was completed before his passing. It seemed to take yet another generation before the book was agreed to be complete. And even then, every couple of generations, there were additions and subtractions from the book.

DR: And did this take place in what was then known as Persia?

DS: *I first see the room, the scribes, the writers, the stories, the papers, some papyrus, sandstone.*

Take me out further than this, let me know exactly where we are please.

We cannot say it was written exclusively in Persia. It does not feel like the origins were started there. The Bible was completed there. It was started someplace smaller, simpler, and then brought to Persia for work with it. So, part of it was in

Persia and the completion of it was in Persia, but it was not started there. It was started as an idea in three or four tribal families, different tribes, three or four families in three or four different tribes. And as they came together, with Ezra, then it was decided this needed to include all. And that it is when it moved to Persia.

DR: Can you see, were these tribes in the north, east, south, west of Persia, ...where it started?

DS: We are seeing northwest, north, northwest, and west. And again, it feels as if there were some exclusions. And it was Ezra that said everyone must be involved, that there are storytellers in every tribe. And that is when they chose Persia to bring all to, and it became a life work.

Some of the scribes stayed there. They did not live there permanently, but they spent more time there than with their family because it became a life project. It did go on for two, maybe three generations.

There were some squabbles, some disagreements, strong disagreements about what the simple truths were. Once Ezra was gone, there were strong disagreements over what the embellishments were and what they were not. Ezra was the last expert, and so there were several meetings, three, five times a year for three generations, finalizing and editing. And then it would be fine for years, and then someone would question, and then they would come together again. So, they came together every five or seven years to review agreement and disagreement.

Just as the storytellers had a line of storytellers, the scribes who were involved with the Bible project, their sons that were inscripted to the next generation of the Bible process. It was really kept in the same families, because they felt it would help with the consistency and the truth. It really was trying to find the simple truths, trying to uncover that which was within the embellishments, what was the real truth, the real story.

Sometimes they got lost in trying to find it, because as we, the Counsel, witnessed the time of Eden and the beginnings, we always held the truth, the simplicity of it. And so, as we witnessed the embellishments and the desire to recover the truth, it was interesting to us to hold witness to what we knew the truths were with what they uncovered. We had no participation or influence in this. It had to be embellished in their own evolutionary way, and it had to be uncovered it its own evolutionary way.

I can feel the Counsel's genuine interest in how these Bible stories "evolved" through the embellishments and back to the truths. It also feels that the Counsel was positively affected by the "simple truths" they witnessed, and they held on to that. I find it fascinating to realize that the Counsel is learning from us as much as serving us.

DR: Was Ezra a scribe and did he know the oral histories himself? Was he trained?

DS: He had the oral histories. He was not a scribe. He was the elder. He did not like the word expert, but we would call him "expert". And for a long time, Ezra was the final word. Upon his passing is when the squabbles began because it was as if there was not another that had his experience and his long life. And so, the simplicity of the truth became harder to find. When Ezra was alive, it was clear.

DR: So, he (Ezra) actually had memorized the oral histories himself?

DS: He was one of the storytellers in his family line, yes.

DR: Were there other important people who could be named and who were part of the process of writing?

There is a long pause here.

DS: Ezra was the lone elder expert. We will not say he lived longer than anyone else, but among the storytellers he was the most respected. There was a lot of squabbles, disagreements. I can feel the certainty of these men. I can feel the dedication of the faithfulness within them, but I cannot give you names.

Each was certain of their truths, were certain their stories were not embellished. And it was only in the telling of the stories that Ezra knew that they could then perceive the embellishments that must have happened in the generations before them. It wasn't that Ezra convinced anyone of the truth. It was the way his story was told that rang true. There was a holiness in the truth of it. And, it feels as if when Ezra left that was gone. Somehow the gathering lost their holiness, and so the certainty of the simple truth became lost, and the purpose became lost. So, I cannot give you names.

Discussion

WHO ACTUALLY WROTE THE HEBREW BIBLE?

You will find a Discussion Section after each chapter in this book. After the channeling was complete, Donna and Dan continued to discuss the channel and Donna continued to explain and share the knowings that she was left with. These sections serve to clarify information of the channel and offer some new information.

#9 Recording 1:36:02 *Storytellers and Oral Tradition*

DR: That's interesting... the whole thing with who wrote the Bible, that's a big controversy. (I show her the cover of the book Who Wrote the Bible by R.E. Friedman)

DS: Fascinating, yes.

DR: So that answered a lot of the questions. First, there is oral history. The oral tradition is bandied about, but no one really knows what it is. And I've read elsewhere where there were speakers who were trained in knowledge and they spent years or decades memorizing.

DS: Yes. But they could also do it more easily than others. That is why there was a line (lineage), because they had the gift of memory from Eden. So, it's like they had shared memories and then it was just to activate the shared memories.

DR: And, because they were so well-trained, it preserved the memories intact for many, many years.

DS: Yes, but then as we evolved and the individuality and the uniqueness evolved, some of the storytellers wanted to embellish. But they couldn't do it till the elder died, because the elder wouldn't have it.

DR: Right, but the point is even if you go a thousand years, two thousand years, if you are able to maintain the core of the story intact...

DS: Exactly, and they did.

DR: And you don't just dismiss it and say, "Oh, oral history. I'm sure after two thousand years…"

DS: Oh, they did. I want to say they never embellished the core. There was a sacredness to the core truths. That is something I would say that your Hebrews have. I don't know anything about it. I am not speaking from any kind of experience. But my experience of the men we have studied, they had such faithful dedication to the core beliefs. And that was passed on.

DR: And Ezra is the name that comes up consistently in the history as the one who had a big part in the writing of the Bible. So that was verified. So that is very consistent. And that is what I am also looking for, consistency.

DS: When the group of men came together to write the Bible, there was always an elder. Each family would send the eldest they had to help to discern truth. And it felt, *perfectly willing to be wrong*, it felt like Ezra was probably one of the last elders. And then after that, there weren't any elders that really had direct experience. It was like there were certain experiences that died with some of them. That is again why I think they lasted so long. They lived long lives.

DR: Yes, but what you get from the Counsel is so much more detailed and in depth, because all that's really known is that there are these men of the Great Assembly in Persia who compiled the book. There are no details, and then you say there are scribes and each family member…

DS: They knew every tribe had the truth. They wanted all the tribal truths to come together and then the common truth would be what the Bible came from. So, the discussions were about the embellishments, "Yes to this. No to that." But the truth was always there. And so, I'm still going to say that this Bible that you are studying contains core truths. That was safeguarded.

DR: Yes, exactly.

DS: Even when they composed stories such as I saw from Joseph, they still maintained the truth of the moment.

DR: Right, the events happened. There were people of that name or that ilk (nature) who actually did something.

DS: Yes.

Section One

ADAM & EVE – NO ORIGINAL SIN

The biblical story of Adam and Eve begins with two versions in the book of Genesis.

And God created man in His image, in the image of God He created him; male and female He created them. (Genesis:1:27)

The LORD God formed man from the dust of the earth. He blew into his nostrils the breath of life, and man became a living being. (Genesis 2:7)

So the LORD God cast a deep sleep upon the man; and, while he slept, He took one of his ribs and closed up the flesh at that spot. And the LORD God fashioned the rib that He had taken from the man into a woman; and he brought her to the man. (Genesis 2: 21-22)

This is a wonderful Biblical story. God creates man, Adam, from dust, and then takes a rib from the man to create a woman, Eve. These are the first humans, and they live in peace and comfort in Eden, until a snake convinces Eve to eat fruit of the Tree of Knowledge of Good and Bad and to give fruit to her husband to eat. Having their eyes opened and disobeying a direct command, they were expelled from Eden.

Now, this story is hard for many today to believe and raises so many questions that are difficult to answer, such as:

- Why didn't God just create Eve from dust like Adam was created?

- Why would God plant a tree that imparted knowledge, then lie that eating it would cause death when it didn't?

- Why wouldn't God want His creations to be knowledgeable and not naive and ignorant?

- Why would an all-powerful God allow the new creations to be compromised, that is, set up for failure by providing temptation?

- Having built a beautiful garden, Eden, why would God insist that it be abandoned and not just correct the errors in the humans that he created?

- If God wanted to populate the Earth with humans, why not make many dozens or more humans at the beginning, so that there would be more genetic variation and a higher population growth rate of the enhanced humans without huge inbreeding issues?

The questions I asked Donna in channel resulted in answers to the questions posed above. They also painted an entirely different picture of the entire story of creation of Adam and Eve, the nature of Eden, the Tree of Life, and the reasons for Adam and Eve to leave the Garden of Eden.

Chapter One

CREATING
ADAM & EVE

#2 Recording 4:45 *Their Mission*

DR: I am going to start with the biblical timeline. Adam and Eve…what was their actual mission in coming to Earth?

DS: There was life on the planet and there needed to be directors of that life. We (the Counsel) saw potential for **exponential** growth, and we were seeding the beings for that growth.

The interaction with the Earth as a being, with the life that was already present, was impacting. And their *mission*, to use your word, was to direct, lead in some way, the growth and changes that we (the Counsel) saw were possible.

There was a sense that their (Adam and Eve) understanding of their mission held true and strong within them. But the longer they were on the planet, the longer they lived in the body, it seemed there was almost a forgetfulness. They never lost awareness of their mission and source, but did lose some of their clarity. As they lost clarity, their mission sometimes became clouded. Even though there was memory of the mission itself, the clarity was lost in the how of it.

#3 Recording 9:14 *Timing of Their Creation*

DR: How long ago did the Adam creation take place? Was this thousands, tens of thousands, or a million years ago?

DS: *Show me the timelines here, please.*

We first witnessed the growth of life on the Earth when consciousness ...*I am not sure that is the right word...* when the brain started to think independently. We paid little attention to the tribal brain, the pack mentality, where the memories are shared.

But when mind started to think individually, our attention was caught.

The sensation is like a scientist discovering something. But we would not call ourselves scientists in the strict use of your word. We wanted to influence that thinking mind, encourage that thinking mind, contribute to what it could think, how it could think, what it could experience. We wanted to contribute to its experiences. We are choosing our words carefully here because, as previously stated, at first, we did not understand EVOLUTION completely as it was on the Earth.

But we saw a thinking mind, thinking individually from individual experiences, and wanted to bestow there different experiences, less natural experiences. And so, the concept of creating Adam would then influence experience; interaction would influence experience.

And so, the time-specific is difficult for us to say. We made the decision based not on time, for we are not of time, but on what we witnessed in the experiences of the separate thinking minds. As those humanoids started to think for themselves and have experiences that they shared, that was when we decided to influence the experiences and the concept of the Adam was created.

[**Note:** The use of 'the' in front of a name is explained in the Introduction on page 8.]

DR: When it was perceived that there was a thinking mind in the humanoids, that's when Adam and Eve were created to help accelerate that process?

DS: Yes. We did not intend acceleration; we intended experiences that would not come from the natural environment, experiences that came from the Adam and the Eve. These experiences were made possible by the presence of Adam and Eve. So, we could insert experiences that did not come from the nature of the planet itself. We were influencing the experiences as an experiment. We had no intention other than to watch the effect.

#9 Recording 37:28 *Creation When Hominids Carried Fire and Made Tools*

DR: So can you tell if this happened say 30 000, 35 000 years ago in our time?

DS: It feels much older than that.

DR: Would it be 100 000 years, 200 000 years?

DS: *How can we give them time to this, please?*

First, I am shown the humanoids, and their primitiveness and their basic use of tools. I can see that fire is present though it is not consistent. It is as if they have not learned how to carry fire. And so, some carry fire and they are luckier than those who do not yet know how to carry fire.

There are tools among the humanoids. There is still development and change occurring in animals. There is a lushness to the Earth, but an unpredictability in her weather systems, in her oceans and lands.

Can we put time frame to this? Can we use years, please?

The Counsel perceives in terms of developments, not in terms of years. And so, when I ask for the time frame, I am told of the tools. It was just at the beginning when they were learning to carry fire; just at the beginning when they were learning to create tools. Such that when Adam and Eve entered the Earth, they had a more sophisticated knowledge of carrying fire and tools. And so, they positively affected creating of tools and carrying of fire.

Show me times frames in terms of years, please.

100 000? 200 000? 300 000?

It feels very uncomfortable to find a date, but as I sense numbers, 300 000 is too far away. It feels as if it is perhaps 100 000 to 200 000, but I am not certain. I do not have a date for this.

[We did not get a satisfactory answer for Adam and Eve time of creation in earth years.]

#2 Recording 9:36 *Creating Adam and Eve on Earth*

DR: Were they, (Adam and Eve), seeded, transported and their bodies created? What was the nature of how they came to Earth?

DS: They were seeded here as a life-force, and then as your mythology tells it, bodies were created. The bodies were created here so that they would be made of the Earth and not made of someplace else. But they came as a life-force. So to use the word *seeded* is appropriate. And then the bodies, that these seeds were placed inside of, were created here.

DR: Does that mean that they were fully functional humans, eating, procreating, everything that a human today does?

DS: They were created in adult form. There was a learning curve of being in the body. But for the most part what you say is accurate. They were human.

DR: Where were they seeded from? Were they brought in or transported from another planet or from where?

DS: There is a lot of reluctance around answering this. *Creator of All That Is, please show me now. It feels dimensional. Clearer please.*

It was an experiment in creation. It comes from a higher level of dimensional space, sixth or seventh dimension. The decision was sharing; it feels like an out-breath, it feels like an experiment. It was an act of creation. And what was created was not as important as the act of creation itself. There is no judgment in the level of creation. This was an experiment at a more sophisticated level of creation, and it had simplicity in it. It was a simple desire to participate with other creations, but from a more sophisticated level.

When I perceive it energetically, we understand the previous answer of them being leaders. They were the most sophisticated creation on the planet, different from the other creations, and so thought to be able to go further, and to create on their own as well. Hence your word *procreation*. The other creations also procreated, but this was a more sophisticated creation. It's interesting, because it feels as if there is an unknown quantity in the creation of them (Adam and Eve).

DR: So was this the first time this had been done where a life force at that level was brought to Earth and then put into a human body? Was that the experiment then? Was this the first time that this had been done successfully?

DS: The first time successfully on the Earth, the first time successfully in the second and third dimensions. For when they were created, Earth was more second dimension, and with their creation it was drawing the Earth into third dimension. It was a science experiment.

Creator of All That Is, show me this please. It's interesting, that I am seeing two levels of answer.

One that feels more like a Counsel of Creators that have a scientific approach. They are beings, but much evolved.

And then I am also seeing another level that is the creative force, the creative energy directed into creation. And there is a consciousness…

I do not know if that is the right word.

But the creative force also participates. It's not just doing as it's ordered; there is participation and there is feedback and understanding. The structures are created by the Counsel, but the creative forces using the Counsel's structures, also created.

So, the Counsel believes they are creating. But in actuality, CREATION is using the Counsel to experiment in creating. So, there are two levels to what we are seeing as it is presented to you. It is science, creating and thinking they are choosing to create, when CREATION is using science to create.

#2 Recording 17:51 *Pair Created with Distinct Differences*

DR: Explain the mythology of Eve being created from Adam.

DS: There was one body, constructed first. We recognized, in science, that we did not want them to be the same. Your word would be *clone*. And so, we took part of the first creation and used that as the seed for the second. But then allowed there to be distinct differences to ensure it was a distinct and separate creation.

There was often in creation, things created in pairs. Not specifically for procreation, but to allow difference, so the two, similar but different, could then be monitored, watched in their evolution. And the distinct differences allowed them to evolve differently, at each level of creation, until we came to the creation of humans.

The CREATION itself, was wanting to witness how two creations, very similar but also distinctly different, could evolve on their own, where that would take them, and so often pairs were created. And the Counsel thought it was their idea when it was CREATION, moving through the Counsel, to orchestrate an evolution. And when one pair were distinctly different, one from the other, EVOLUTION could truly be witnessed.

#2 Recording 20:55 *First Body Androgynous; Second Body from Cells, Not Rib*

DR: What part of Adam was used to create Eve and was it in that order, first male, then female?

DS: The first body created was androgynous. In creating the second, part of the distinct difference was the creation of the male to female, and from CREATION, the god and goddess, the male and the female, the thinking compared to the feeling. And so, the difference in gender was a way of marking their difference, and then also to ensure that procreation could occur. There was a question whether the procreation would occur, and so they were created so that it was possible, but whether it would happen was not clear.

The myth of the rib of Adam feels to be more because the

cells of the marrow in the bone were part of the basic recipe of the second body. But the DNA was altered, and the energy brought into the body was altered.

Again, I feel this science council, in an experiment on the Earth and creation energies, using the science council to evolve so much more than another life form. As if there was a science experiment on the planet Earth by a species. But also, creation forces using inspired ideas to the science forces to experiment so much further than they realized.

[**Note from Dan:** *This was a marvelous and unexpected finding, that marrow cells from the rib, and not a whole rib, was used to help create the second body for Eve. This was an extremely scientific explanation as marrow cells can be used to create almost any other type of cell in the body unlike all other cells which are fixed as to tissue type, and can't change later into any other kind of cell.*]

#2 Recording 24:26 *Creation an Experiment, Two Halves of a Whole but Distinct Differences*

DR: So, the human body that was created from the life force was at first androgynous and then basically split in two, into male and female? It was almost a split, rather than one created from the other, or....

DS: One was created, and it was androgynous; and then there was the inspiration to create a second. Part of the first body, feels like bone marrow, was used, with alterations. And that is when the concept of procreation, male-female, *though I am not sure those were the words used,* was born. So, one was not really made from the other, but the seed of the second body came from the marrow of the first, and then it was created separately.

It felt important to the experiment and <u>very</u> important to CREATION itself, that there was a distinct difference in this pair. Even more so than other pairs that had been created. It was almost like a graduation, on a science level, of CREATION with how different the pairs could be.

The humans were the graduation of creation for the Counsel, and for CREATION itself, an experimentation with what we would call male-female energy. But it was ordered in such a way that the Counsel could not anticipate where this would go, because CREATION itself did not want to plan where this would go. It was a sense of a freedom to evolve. And so, the energies wanted to be similar, but also distinctly different; two halves of the same whole, but also distinctly different... harmonious, but different. <u>And from the Counsel's perspective, this was the graduation of creation. They created animals or insects or other lower-level creations, and then the human creation was the graduation of it.</u>

<u>#2 Recording 27:07</u> *Experiment Imparting Higher Consciousness*

DR: There were already humanoids, humans on Earth that were male and female, at a lower level, correct?

*[**Note:** The more accepted anthropological term is 'hominids', but we started with humanoids and so continue with that term.]*

DS: I want to say yes and no.

The distinction was not as different. These beings (Adam and Eve) were more evolved. It was where the humanoids would have come in time, but this accelerated the process. And so, the distinction was not as strong in the humanoids.

There was procreation, but without consciousness. There were the glimmers of consciousness. But Adam and Eve had consciousness. Adam and Eve had distinct awareness of their differences and had the beginnings of choice. It doesn't feel like choice was there, but there was more choice in these creations than there was in the humanoids.

The humanoids were more instinctive, and procreation was to prevent extinction. It was instinctive within them. It was survival. Consciousness was starting to evolve within them, but the consciousness was implanted at a much more evolved rate with those which were named Adam and Eve.

At this point, I can see, and am sensing both humanoid and the Adam and Eve creation. I feel the distinct difference in consciousness between the two and I can sense that if the humanoids were left alone to evolve, they would have achieved a form of consciousness eventually.

When we speak about "choice", I feel the conscious awareness that Adam and Eve have, and that this conscious awareness enabled them to have active choice. I see how the humanoids are more instinctive and reactive and choice is as a result of instinctive reaction. Whereas with the Adam and Eve, there is more thought, more proactive awareness, and so their choices hold more free will. Their choices are not as instinctively reactive as the humanoids. The humanoids feel slower in thought to me. Adam and Eve, their thought processes are more clear, more cognizant.

Here again the use of the "the" in front of the reference to Adam and Eve. When we use the word "the" before the names of Adam and Eve, it is because we are sensing the original signature and so the identity is not as such as humans would know. It is as if the name is

46

simply the label for that original creation that becomes Adam and Eve. In this reference, Adam and Eve are not yet in their human identities.

*[**Note:** It almost seems like the Biblical eating of the fruit and their eyes being opened is an explanation for being created with higher consciousness, and having free will and choice.]*

#3 Recording 18:20 *Creation Process Used Earth Elements; Body Came to Life When the Soul Entered the Body*

DR: As a scientist, I am very curious about the process that was used to create the first androgynous body. Is it possible to give me some more explanation of how that was created? Was it from a single cell that was grown into a body, or the DNA used?

DS: The body was created from elements, and we use the word elements in a chemical way, elements from the Earth itself. It was important that this body was of the Earth and not of us. It was important that it would fit in with the Earth, would need what the Earth has, would breathe what the Earth breathes, and would live as the Earth lives. And so, its chemicals, its chemistry came from the Earth elements. We had access to varying forms, animals, humanoids, that had evolved. Though at this point, we did not understand EVOLUTION. We simply saw the various creatures on the planet and took from them.

Since I have limited science knowledge, I do not have the language nor the knowledge to answer this question in the way that Dan has posed it. It has been my experience as a channel, that whatever energies we are channeling, they are using our experience, our knowledge to deliver their messages. I believe this is what creates such variation in channeled information.

The experience of the channel, if it is varied, provides more to work with. I believe that if I had a science education, as Dan has, I would have been better able to deliver the answer to this question as it is asked. The limitation of this answer is my limitation, not the Counsel's.

The process I cannot see. I see that the creation came to life when the soul occupied it. And the Counsel says, "The creation body of Adam did not come to life until the soul occupied it. That is our (the Counsel's) belief, which was how we create.

Understand, we did not, at that creation point, truly did not understand EVOLUTION as the Earth evolves. We did understand the connection or saw the connection between the creatures and the planet herself. We saw the ties energetically. We saw the inter-dependencies. We saw how each served the other. We saw the harmony between all of the creatures but had not yet realized that the harmony of all the creatures on the planet came because each was an evolved version of their previous self. We had not recognized that yet.

It was only when Adam evolved that our attention was drawn to EVOLUTION. We simply saw the creatures; we had not monitored their creation. We simply witnessed these creatures that were interconnected and had energetic bonds and physical dependencies and served one another. And so, we took from their chemistries that which created the body of Adam. And then the soul is what made it Adam, is what brought it to life."

Does this answer you?

I can feel the amazement of the Counsel at the EVOLUTION present on the Earth. They truly had no idea that there was the instinct to evolve present on the Earth. I am grateful that the Counsel is very willing for me to witness their lack of understanding and share it with you. The Counsel is truly open for us to understanding their experiment and their intention with it.

DR: Not exactly. I am not sure that you have the answer. I am just curious about the cells, living cells, biological material from the humanoids and other living beings were they actually used in the construct?

DS: Yes. We wanted the creature we were creating to be connected to these creatures, to be harmonized with these creatures. We wanted these creatures to recognize themselves in what we were creating. We did not want "us" on the planet. We wanted something of them on the planet. And so, it was important that the body of Adam was of the Earth.

DR: Were there cells, for example, from the humanoids that were used to create a similar type, similar looking being to the humanoids?

DS: Yes, and then there were qualities from some of the others. I am not seeing and cannot identify.

There is just this sense of harvesting? And I don't know if it is cells or DNA. I don't know what I am seeing. But there was a sense that ...

The sense is that the body must be of the Earth and then the soul occupies the body, and that's what brought it to life.

Again, I struggle to understand what I see as the Counsel answers this question about the science of it. I sense what I call "harvesting" but I have very little science knowledge and so I do not have the words or the understanding to describe what this answer is. Since I do not "know", I then move into what I call sensing and get a feel for how this creation was accomplished. This is where the word "harvesting" comes from. This is my word, not a word from the Counsel. It is the word I am using to describe what I can sense or feel as I attempt to witness the answer to this question. Again, my limited science knowledge is what limits this answer here.

I see that the Counsel genuinely wanted to add to the Earth something that was from the Earth. They were attempting to accelerate the growth potential of a creature of Earth. It was fascinating how important this was to them.

DR: And then there was DNA manipulation of the body before it was inhabited, before it was brought to life. So, there was some DNA manipulation done in the process?

DS: **Counsel objects to your word manipulation.** There is a negative connotation to it; they object to it. *And if not manipulation, what word?* It is as if the word that is acceptable is created, not manipulated.

There was inspiration in the creation; there was some experimentation in the creation. The intent was pure. There was no selfish purpose to this. It served experience, but there was no selfishness in it. We did not have a specific goal other than to have this creature be of the Earth, connected to others that are there, recognized by others that were already there and able to recognize those that were there.

50

We did not want this creature to feel like it did not belong. We did not want this creature to be alien in any way. We wanted this creature to be recognized by the creatures that were there and recognize the creatures that were there. And so, the DNA manipulation, to use your term, was more about familiarity, more to breed familiarity, more to, there is no other word. In other words, Adam did not have to name the animals, he knew the animals. The animals knew Adam, even though he might be new, he was recognizable to them, and they were recognizable to him. So, there was a harmony. We did not want to disturb the harmony of the planet. We wanted to insert for experience. But we did not want to disturb the harmony. And so, the harmony was what was needed to be maintained.

[**Note:** *The Discussion section, #4 Recording 1:00:56 Discussion Creating Adam and Eve on page 118 finally answers Dan's question as to how the bodies were created in a laboratory-type setting.*]

#3 Recording 13:44 *Souls of Adam and Eve*

DR: The Adam and Eve, was it one soul that inhabited both those created bodies or two different souls that inhabited those two different created bodies?

DS: Two different souls. When we are at the point of that creation of Adam and Eve, first one soul, Adam, and there was exhilaration, freedom, and a loneliness. We, the soul, experienced the form of Adam, and there was a separation there. The soul was still available to us and us to it, but in the creation of the human Adam, there was a loneliness that was not anticipated. Another decision was made, about the creation of Eve, to aid … *no, wrong word…* to answer, to answer that loneliness. So, a second soul occupied the creation of Eve. Interesting, that the second soul also experienced loneliness. But in their togetherness, in their openness to each other, the loneliness was greatly reduced. And so, we understood, oneness, separateness, aloneness in a different way.

Here I am present to the creation and can feel the separation and the resulting loneliness. Through my channeling connection, I am blended with the Counsel through this creative process. I can sense that they are "as one" in the first stages of the creation of Adam. And then, as Adam becomes more human, that is when I can feel the separation they speak of. I can actually feel it and it leaves within me an understanding of separation that I had never experienced before.

It touches my heart, and I can feel that the Counsel also felt that loneliness and wanted to answer it. I can also feel that it was interesting to them that when Eve was created, loneliness again resulted and so as it is said, their understanding of oneness and separateness deepened. It is fascinating to experience the growth and learning of the Counsel as they move through this process of creating the Adam and the Eve.

DR: Was there a name for the soul that became Eve? Was it Lilith?

DS: We would say no. There was a sense of non-identity to the soul. It was not incarnated before. It was raw potential. And that in and of itself produced another experiment; that this raw potential would have its first experience in incarnated form, in the form of Eve. It would be uninfluenced by us in any way, uninfluenced by any previous incarnations. It is raw soul essence, raw potential, and that aided and affected the dance between the Adam and the Eve.

Adam had memories that Eve did not have. Eve had clarity and freedom, unencumbered by memories that added a whole dynamic to the creation, the experiment. So, the answer to your question is no.

[**Note:** *More information is available about Eve, her soul, life and death can be found in* <u>Women of the Hebrew Bible: Their Stories</u> *(Ronis and Somerville, 2024)*]

#3 Recording 27:17 *Differences Between Adam and Eve*

DS: When we realized that the soul of Adam influenced Adam more than we expected, we decided that Eve would not have that influence. And so, Adam had memories at a soul level. Eve did not. It is as if Eve was a new soul.

And so, there are more memories in your male gender that in your female gender. The female gender is more free of memory. We do not say they are free of memory now; they most certainly are not. But in its initiation, the female was free of memory.

The Counsel's use of the word memories here is fascinating. I can sense that the word refers to a soul memory that came into the Adam upon being brought to life. Those "soul memories" then affected and influenced Adam in his choices and viewpoints. I cannot see the memories; neither can I sense what those memories are or how they influenced. I can simply feel the Counsel as they realized that the memories were/would affect Adam in his behaviour and choices. I can witness the Counsel as they saw that influence and then made a decision – a scientific decision – that Eve was to be different.

Also, I can sense the importance of the difference between Adam and Eve, at the soul level, with these memories. I can sense where the memories of Adam will lead, and where the clarity of Eve will take her. I perceive the difference of male and female being created and the importance of this amazingly simple decision that Eve would be of an unencumbered soul, free of memories. I can also perceive how this will affect Eve and how that will come to affect females in human form over time. As if with this simple decision, I can see how it will lead to an evolutionary difference between men and women over time.

DR: How were these sex differences created if the first body was androgynous? Was that through DNA?

DS: The recognition of procreation, the decision to create that which was needed for procreation, we again witnessed the creatures already present and adapted that.

Understood?

DR: Yes. So that was then added from what the creatures had, which created their sexual differences?

DS: Yes, it was about procreation, and so it was about the seeds. How are the seeds carried? How are the seeds fertilized? But we wanted some uniqueness to it. And we were dealing with the loneliness of <u>the</u> Adam. There was a recognition in the loneliness of Adam entering form that we wanted to allow.

We wondered if we could allow relationship, if we could make the procreation a method, if it could be less animalistic and more… something else. And so, there were adaptations made to the procreation. *It is confusing. Relationship is the wrong word.*

Initially, copulation was purely for procreation. But the loneliness that occurred affected the procreation. There were times the procreation was and still can be animalistic and instinctive. But we wanted consciousness ... *There it is. That is the right word.* We wanted <u>consciousness</u> connected to the instinctive procreation. Because that was the purpose, to introduce a consciousness. And so, we wanted the consciousness to differentiate the humans from the animals, and we wanted consciousness involved in procreation.

So, there are times in procreation it would be for survival. They must procreate to survive. But there was also potential in the consciousness for it to be more than just procreation. We did not know what that would become. But we wanted to differentiate. We wanted the consciousness that was seeded in Adam and Eve to be different from the animalistic natural instinct. We wanted the consciousness to intertwine with the natural instinct. And that is how Adam and Eve became <u>humans</u>, not humanoids. There were distinct differences that the consciousness provided.

And so, the procreation was designed to procreate. But the consciousness allowed the procreation to be different, because that consciousness was not present in the creatures. So, they were driven by instinct only. We wanted Adam and Eve to be driven by instinct and consciousness. We did not design what that drive would be, but we wanted connection, so we did make connections.

You might again use manipulation as your word, but it wasn't our intention to manipulate. It was to connect consciousness to instinct and instinct to consciousness, so that they were not separate from one another.

As consciousness is explained by the Counsel, I can very clearly feel a distinct difference between it and instinctive procreation. In consciousness there is more awareness, more choice, and more understanding. In instinct, it is driven, without thought or reason. There is an absence of reason all together.

The Counsel is direct, adamant, in their intent to bring a different level of consciousness to the Earth.

The Counsel is clear, and scientific and it truly drives them in their creation of Adam and Eve; and continues to affect them in creating an Adam and Eve in regard to procreation. Here the Counsel feels very scientific and noticeably clear in what they are doing and how they are doing it.

When it comes to procreation, the Counsel take their creation a step further by bringing consciousness to instinctive procreation. It is fascinating to feel the full effect of an open consciousness being created within Adam and Eve. I can feel the power of it and the unknown quantity in it. The Counsel is experimenting, creating and scientific in that creation.

I can feel the potential as they bring consciousness to instinctive procreation. That consciousness has the capacity for <u>*patience, compassion, and awareness*</u> *of the sharing in procreation, all of which is absent with instinctive procreation. The consciousness creates a space for awareness and connection, and this is where the Counsel is truly creating something new on the planet. And as I view this, I feel how it can, and will, expand and where it can take the human species.*

DR: So, this was more of wanting to see if they could create a bond, a feeling that was different from just animal coupling.

DS: Yes. We had witnessed it in some of your creatures. But the consciousness that we intended to place on the Earth was much more evolved than the care of a mother lion for her cub. And so, we simply connected, *it's the only word I can use*, connected the consciousness to the instincts of procreation and the instincts of natural protection, preservation, to the consciousness. <u>When we made the connection, we didn't design what that would do.</u> We made the connection like you would connect the wires and then let the engines run. We attempted as little manipulation, *this is why they do not like the word*, as little manipulation as we could. We were creating. We wanted an experiment. We wanted to make a difference. We wanted to insert into the planetary space. It was well intended.

Here I can sense it was all science. They are not trying to create "love," but are taking the caring and protective consciousness of the animals and then connecting consciousness to it and letting it grow; letting it move naturally to the next level.

There is also a sense that the Counsel is not exactly sure how this will turn out, but their intent is clear. And so, adding consciousness to procreation – like attaching two wires in an engine – allows that insertion to move to another level. I can feel their detachment when this insertion is made. They really do simply "connect the wires" and leave the engine to run.

Chapter Two

ADAM & EVE
IN EDEN

#2 Recording 32:41 *Garden of Eden*

DR: The myth of the Garden of Eden, how does that relate to what actually happened?

DS: There was a protected space when the beings that seeded Adam and Eve arrived. It was an energetic protection, and it held, and was decided to be released when the continents, the plates, broke. Eden was requiring too much energy to protect where the offspring went. Once the plates split, there was a sense of evolution far beyond the creatures. And the Counsel then decided to let the experiment direct itself.

Again, at the level of CREATION, there was an inspiration for freedom because the protection (of Eden) had limited the response and growth. And so, the inspirations to let the protection of the Garden of Eden go allowed for evolution and the birth of choice, because in Eden, there was no need for choice. But without Eden, without that protection, choices had to be made. Learnings began. And the experiment began to be truly experimental.

We have mentioned both CREATION and the Counsel several times now and I wanted to explain the difference that I perceived between the Counsel and CREATION itself.

The Counsel feels to me to be a group of beings that have some separated form but are not human or humanoid. They have one mind. They are of a higher vibration than Earth.

CREATION is that place from which the raw potential for creating comes. It is not truly "thinking" or cognizant as we know those words as humans. But once creating has begun, that creation then catches the focus of CREATION itself and CREATION then adds its inspirations and impulses to the created idea through the one bringing a new creation into being.

One could almost use CREATION and Creator of All That Is synonymously, but not exactly. As I feel a difference in their vibration. Creator is slightly less in vibration, more cognizant and has a more god-like sensations in its vibration. Whereas CREATION feels more like pure potential to me; I can sense no agenda, no commands, and no demands. Here all I sense is simply in the joy of something being brought into form as a creation.

Creator of All That Is is a creation and originated in CREATION.

Creator of All That Is maintains a strong similarity to CREATION in its vibration and energy. Creator of All that Is is supportive, open, and available, but it is in a form. It is no longer pure potential, but instead potential with direction.

Creator of All That Is is closer in vibration and energy to CREATION than to anything else existing here on the Earth, as I sense the nature of the vibrations.

#2 Recording 7:34 *Timeline, Location*

DR: Is it possible to get a timeline of when these events occurred in Earth's history? And a location, where they came to Earth to do their mission?

DS: This is difficult for the Earth did not look as she looks now. She did not resonate as she resonates now. But in an attempt to answer your question, we would say that they were first close to the equator and in well-vegetated land, almost jungle-like.

*[**Note:** Timelines in terms of human-denominated years are difficult to obtain as the Counsel appears to measure or notice Earth events in terms of human advancements in thinking patterns and not in Earth year chronology. This is better explained in the following passages which were recorded at a later date.]*

#9 Recording 46:00 *The Timeframe of Eden*

DR: How long did Eden persist?

DS: The Counsel likes this question.

Eden was a long timing in our preserved space. We kept the Adam and the Eve protected in the early stages of growth and violence of the evolution. We did not know it as evolution, at the time; we know the word now.

The beginnings of the Earth were violent. The beginning of the creatures was violent. But within Eden, there was a timelessness; there was no aging.

The Counsel has pride in this Eden and its timelessness.

We maintained the freedom of time in the Eden.

We came to the Earth as she was dividing and settling within herself and kept Adam and Eve, the Adam and the Eve in the Eden, until the humanoids were less violent, more cooperative.

We would say the Eden lasted hundreds of years. *A thousand years?* Yes. *Two thousand years?* Yes. *Ten thousand years?* Yes. *Fifty thousand years?* No.

To give an exact time is so difficult because the Counsel merely witnessed the growth of the Earth, the growth of the creatures on the Earth. They waited until what Adam and Eve represented in consciousness could be inserted into the changing Earth in the most viable way.

And so I'm shown that time is when the humanoids had learned how to carry fire and how to make tools, not sophisticated tools, but the beginnings of toolmaking. You see to release Adam and the Eve sooner than that would make them affect, so adversely, the change. We needed to come to a time when the Earth was changing in a way that they could change with her. We could not have them influence toolmaking until toolmaking had begun. We could not have them influence the carrying of fire until the carrying of fire had begun. And so we were very much monitoring Earth and her creations to choose when we could release Adam and Eve. We did release them sooner than when we wanted to. We intended another thousand years or more. But when we realized that they could miss their opportunities for being part of the changing Earth, we had to abandon our plan for the Earth's own changings.

#9 Recording 41:41 *Generations Adam to Abraham for Timing of Eden*

DR: What about the generations from Adam and Eve to Abraham?

DS: The Counsel likes this idea. The Counsel does not like time. The Counsel likes the generations.

Might we see the generations please, between Adam and Eve and Abraham? So that I can count them please.

It is interesting how the generations are being counted, as if the generations are very connected to the evolutionary times and what the Counsel witnessed. At each number we give you, there was some developmental witness that the Counsel took note of. The generational time was important in the evolution of mankind.

Fifteen generations from Adam, then twenty-one generations from Adam, then twenty-eight generations from Adam, thirty-four generations from Adam, fifty-two generations from Adam. Now we are close to the time of tribes that you know of Abraham. It is worth remarking upon that there was not much change between the thirty-two and fifty-two generations. There were not many developments that were noteworthy to the Counsel. This be the best that we can offer to you. Does it serve?

DR: Are those numbers the sum of the generations, or is fifty-two the total number of generations between Adam and Abraham?

DS: Abraham was among the fifty-second to fifty-fifth generation from Adam, but keeping in mind that the generations were not 60 years long. At that stage of mankind there were longer lifetimes.

#2 Recording 7:46 *Timeline, Location*

DS: Timeline is more difficult. As we perceive it, what I am seeing is before the continents broke into the formation of how they are now.

Can you show me the timelines of the breaking of the continents in relationship to them, please? Show me now.

There were warnings issued of the continental breaks, and so they moved several times so as to be in the safest place possible during the continental breaks.

[Note: This statement was initially confusing to me as the large-scale tectonic plate movement is believed to have occurred well before even the earliest of humanoids existed. Again, later recordings

clarified this statement as shown in the following passage.]

#9 Recording 29:49 *Eden – Tectonic Plate Movement*

DR: Let's switch back to Eden.

DS: *One moment, show me... proceed.*

DR: With Eden there was an indication that the tectonic plates were moving and endangered Eden. And this is a question in my mind, because when the tectonic plates really moved fast that was millions or tens of millions of years ago. I don't believe Eden was that long ago and Adam and Eve that long ago. So, can that be better explained?

DS: When the tectonic plates shifted, continents were created. Once that occurred there were still subterranean shifts in the plates as the Earth settled into her new form. There were earthquakes and eruptions. So even though the plates were established, they were not fully settled at their deepest levels. The molten core of the Earth was still finding its center and movement in the subterranean levels of the plates was still active. So even if at the surface there seemed to be stability, there were years of instability for as long as a decade, and then it would go stable and quiet again for several decades. Then it would be unstable for two or three years and then it would grow quiet again.

The tectonic movement was at the subterranean level, closer to the core. The feeling we have is that the Earth herself was settling into her new form, was settling into the place where there would be water and where there would be land. The Earth herself was finding her way to her new shape and form. She was finding her poles; she was finding her center. And, as this occurred, there were earthquakes, tsunamis, and volcanoes.

In exploring the movement of the tectonic plates, I come into the beingness of the Earth herself, and can feel her as a being of great growth and power. I can feel the changes that happen at this time are actually the Earth coming into herself. In this moment, the Earth is a being who is stretching and growing much like someone waking from a good night's sleep.

I can feel the Earth as she is finding her poles and her center, again just like a human finding their sense of balance, their sense of knowing themselves. In this, for me, Earth is so alive, and I am perceiving her and "Recording" her like any other being I have been privileged to be one with through these channelings. And in my Recording of Earth at this time, my sense of the Earth is as this being who is discovering itself. Earth is alive, she feels the movement of the waters and the stillness of her lands. She feels the molten power in her core. She feels alive and her "settling into herself" is her exploration of her own aliveness. In this connection to the Earth, I am one with her as she grows and moves in her growth. Fascinating to feel the Earth like this.

The image we have when we ask to see the destruction of Eden is of an earthquake that destroys a wall of sorts, as if Eden was in this protected place. We are going to call it a wall of stone, and it is cracked and destroyed with an earthquake. Not so much that Eden is destroyed, but the safety of Eden is jeopardized. The energetic holding that we had of Eden could not be anchored solidly into the Earth, because the surface of the Earth needed to have pliability so that as the subterranean levels shifted and the Earth found her new place to be, at the surface everything could still move.

I do see walls of stone and can watch as those walls are weakened and split by earthquake. But the destruction is so much more than the walls splitting and stones tumbling. There is also a weakening of these anchors that hold Eden in place on the Earth and it becomes very difficult for the Counsel to hold the Eden in place through these Earth changes. Amazing to "see" all that holds Eden in her protected place on the Earth.

#2 Recording 45:15 *Tree of Life*

DR: Can you explain the mythology of the Tree of Life and the Tree of Knowledge of Good and Bad, especially the Tree of Life, in the Garden?

DS: We held connection to the natural world on the Earth, for we recognized evolution occurring in the natural world. And the Tree of Life was our connection to Nature, to the natural world of the Earth.

We attempted to involve, *not the right word,* include the natural elements of the Earth herself, in our creations of the humans. And so, the Tree of Life is a wondrous phrase because the natural elements were included in the life we created.

We aimed at harmony between the creations, humans, and the natural elements. We wanted to harmonize with the natures. And so, to harmonize with the natures, we used elements from nature. And we came to recognize this fueled the very **evolution** we did not anticipate, because it was Earth's nature to evolve. It was already in its own process of evolution when we added our creations, the species of humans. We strove not to interfere. We used elements of the nature, hence the Tree of Life.

DR: It was or wasn't an actual thing or creation, or biological organism? Did it have a reality, a substance?

DS: It was a term coined by a human trying to understand our experiment. If we answer you specifically, there was no tree, but the symbolic representation of the Tree of Life was that from the nature of Earth herself. Those evolving creations on Earth became part of the cellular structure that was put into the human creations, so as to harmonize with nature and its evolutionary nature itself. Understood?

DR: Not exactly, but it may not be able to be explained in terms I can understand.

So, there were some cellular structures that harmonized. Did they give off energy or sustenance? Was there an energetic structure that helped sustain Adam and Eve?

DS: There was life on your planet when we created the humans. There was growing life. There were cells that were splitting and becoming something else. There was life and there was the planet herself.

We wanted our beings (the humans) to harmonize with what the planet herself was. And so, we sampled from the planet herself. We sampled from cells that were alive, cells that were splitting and creating, cells that were of the animals, of the insects, of the amoeba, of the growth – anything that was alive and growing. This is what we sampled and adjusted, transformed, as we created the humans. There were humanoids there; there were animals there. And so, we sampled some of them. They were the Tree of Life, because we didn't want to interfere with the harmony of what was being created. We didn't want to create something that could not get along with, communicate with, the life that was already there. We did not want it to be alien! We wanted it to be of the Earth. And so, to make it of the Earth, we made it of the Earth. And when this story was explained, the phrase "Tree of Life" was coined to understand what we were doing.

Does this make this more clear?

DR: Yes, it's starting to be clearer.

DS: It was more to make our creations truly humans of the Earth. We wanted to eliminate anything alien in the body. We wanted the bodies to be of the Earth. We did not want the bodies to be of where we are. We wanted them to be of the Earth, so we used the Earth like a raw material.

And we used different cells from different alive beings, plants, animals, insects there, and did our best not to interfere with their present state of evolution. But what we did not see, and only saw later, was that there is within the cells of Earth and nature, a **"Call to Evolve"**. It is why your dinosaurs created, and then died. It is how different animals adapt to different circumstances.

The Earth and Nature have within its creation the ability to evolve. And so, when we took of the Earth to make our beings we called human (you've called Adam and Eve) we didn't realize there was an evolutionary gene, though it was not a gene … this evolutionary piece. Embedding it into our beings called human, **they** also would be able to evolve.

As I tell you this story, I am immediately aware that CREATION *knew of that possibility. The Counsel did not. **But CREATION did.***

And again, there is this sense of an experiment being created by these beings of the Counsel, inspired by CREATION. But CREATION was very aware that in inspiring them to use parts of the Earth to create the human beings of Earth, the evolutionary bit would be there. And that would allow the humans to evolve as the animals did. It would allow the humans to adapt.

CREATION knew this but neither CREATION nor the Counsel anticipated how the ability to evolve would give way to judgment, to a thinking mind, to directing, to controlling. Because evolution leads to change. But then there are reactions to change. When the tadpole loses its tail and becomes a frog, there is not enough consciousness to judge that evolution. In the humans we created, there was enough consciousness to judge their own evolution. And therein is your problem on the planet, but therein is the amazing miracle of Earth.

#1 Recording 38:52 *Eve Did Not Sin*

*[This is an excerpt from **Women of the Hebrew Bible: Their Stories**]*

DR: Will you explain the myth of Eve eating the forbidden fruit and giving some to Adam, that is in the Bible?

DS: This is connected to the starvation, the meat eating, and the harvesting of animals. We would say to you that what is called in your myth, the apple, is meat. The evil of it was the killing of the animal, making the needs of men's hunger more important than the animal's presence. That was first seen as evil, *that's not the right word,* but it was shocking. That's the word! It was shocking. When there was starvation Adam was desperate and so he killed a live animal, a live healthy animal, roasted the meat, ate some of it raw. But that seemed to create sickness, so then it was cooked. And it feels to us that it was Adam's doing, not Eve's. The children were sick. They were starving, and Eve was with child and starving. Adam flew into a rage of fear. It was in the cold and there were no plants to harvest; the ice, there was no fish to fish. So Adam, in a fury, killed a live, healthy animal. And what later became your Myth of Evil, the Knowledge of Good and Evil, was the knowledge of making man's needs more important than anything else.

The killing, the selfish need answered, but his family survived. There was shame in him, for having killed such a healthy animal. They had not deliberately killed a healthy animal so viciously before.

They had taken the weak ones from the herd. They had taken the young ones, deformed, from the herd. They had eaten meat, but this was decisive, deliberate, and it was the state of the health of the animal. Also, because the animals had not been hunted, the animal did not know to run.

The animal was the victim of Adam and that was the grain, the seed, of what later became your Myth of Evil. It was a selfish act for selfish need. It feels to us that it occurred with Adam to ensure the survival of his family.

How did this become put upon the shoulders of Eve, please show me now?

There was such shame in Adam afterwards, the emotional hurt

we spoke of. It was deep in him, and Eve could feel it and see it. **We want to say being with child she was even more sensitively aware to his shame and his hurt and we want to say to you that we witnessed Eve take the blame. She told Adam that she was the one that called him to do it so that the children would survive, so that the unborn child would survive. She offered to him that when others asked, he could tell them it was for her; it was her that needed, her that asked, her that demanded.**

Adam never used the word demand, but the story did begin that it was Eve's idea to kill a healthy animal, to victimize such an animal. **And it came to be put upon the shoulders of Eve by Eve's own agreement. It was her effort to take some of Adam's shame away.** She was able to convince him that it was her and her children that needed it and so it was her to blame. In his hurtfulness he could accept that. But when we looked inside him there was still a grain that he always knew the truth, but it was not spoken.

I cannot see how the tree or the apple or the snake come into being.

Though when we explore the snake, it is lies, cheating, murderous intent of taking the animal's life. But I cannot see how this became a snake.

DR: This happened after leaving Eden?

DS: Yes, because there was no possibility of starvation in Eden. It was after Eden.

Chapter Three

OTHER PAIRS

#4 Recording 4:00 *Three Other Pairs Created in Eden*

DR: How large was the group just before they left Eden?

DS: I want to say six or eight, but it feels more like eight. When they left Eden, they moved in different directions, in pairs.

Not certain, six or eight. Why is there this discrepancy? Show me now, please.

There were three pairs plus Adam and Eve. That's why six then eight. There are three pairs plus Adam and Eve which equals the eight.

DR: Who were the others?

DS: **Other created beings.** Others created by us to affect the entire planet. The success of the first two allowed us, encouraged us, to create others.

Adam and Eve hold more strength, more power because they were the first. We adapted and made changes as we created the next pairs. The next pairs were created because of the scope of the planet. That we wanted to have effects elsewhere. The three other pairs were basically the same as Adam and Eve, but with some small changes from what we had learnt from the creation of Adam and Eve. **So, four pairs left Eden, and all in different directions.**

DR: Are there names for these other six beings?

DS: It feels as if the other six beings are quieter.

[We learned from the stories that arose through the Jesus, through the Adam and Eve stories and so, there are not names for us to give you. When the Jesus story occurred, the history was investigated. Adam and Eve became someone they weren't meant to be as well. And so, we wished the others to remain nameless and discreet. And so, there are not names for us to give you.]

DR: Did these eight go off in pairs, four pairs?

DS: Yes, four pairs in different directions.

DR: In four different directions?

DS: Yes.

It is important here to say that even though the Counsel created Adam and Eve, because of their "no time" space that they inhabit, they have/had access to the Jesus stories, meaning they can move through time and space to see how the Jesus stories unfolded and their full impact on our world. I can feel their disquiet at the importance that both Jesus and Adam and Eve acquired in our history. There is a strong sense that the Counsel does not want such as thing to happen again, and so, they flatly refuse to name the other pairs created in order to prevent further importance being laid upon those other pairs.

More information regarding the three other pairs can be found in our first published work Women of the Hebrew Bible: Their Stories.

Chapter Four

OFFSPRING

#9 Recording 50:05 *Procreation and Leaving Eden*

DR: So did Adam and Eve have lots of children, generations of children in Eden?

DS: No, no. We kept them as they were, in the potential of <u>the</u> Adam and <u>the</u> Eve. **We did not insert procreation in Eden (until near the very end).** It was the last insertion in their programming. And so they were ageless, timeless, learning, growing, understanding, training to the Earth herself, but in our timeless environment.

For thousands of years they were just themselves. They were not the humans they became. This was just the beginnings.

Just as we had decided that it was time to release the Eden before it was truly destroyed, the last insertion was procreation. And there was one generation born in Eden and then Eden was destroyed. Thus, the third generation was born outside of Eden. But there were still strong memories and training from Eden.

When Adam and Eve left Eden their children were with them, and their children were perhaps late teens. They carried timelessness with them, so they lived longer, even on the Earth, longer, and still stayed to themselves, creating first their own tribe, before they were found by other humanoids. They kept to themselves.

And I am guessing, this is thousands of years. They are in timelessness. They are in their own form of Eden now on the Earth, not that preserved of space of the Counsel. The Counsel has freed them. But they come into the Earth with such knowledge and such patterns of behaviour that they hold this for thousands of years.

Their procreation is not comparable in years to what it is now where your generation would be a hundred years. So it is hard to put time to this. It feels like the first generation from Adam and Eve was a thousand years old, two thousand years old, before they were at the mature state of considering family and procreation. Everything was very stretched out, timeless, as if they had left Eden, but had not entered the time of the Earth. They were still separate from the Earth in that way.

#2 Recording 35:26 *Enhanced Consciousness*

DR: So, did the offspring of Adam and Eve carry this enhanced consciousness? Was that passed on to them?

DS: Yes, that continued for several generations... I want to say two or three. But as choices were needed to be made, judgments were needed to be made, it did erode the higher consciousness and that is when the experiment really proved interesting.

It was, in fact, curious to the Counsel to watch the higher consciousness lose some of its hold. Such had not been witnessed before and was very enlightening. There was, is, a sense of excitement when the Counsel is allowed to speak of it to you. It was amazing to witness this.

I sense that evolution is being demonstrated through this developing judgment, and in the larger picture, I feel what this means for mankind as a whole. Mankind needed to judge for their safety and survival. This introduces to our consciousness something that was not there before, something more provoked by thought than instinct. I can sense its potential growth and how it evolved into what we are today. It is as if judgment for safety got away from us and continued to evolve on its own, expanding the definition of what "safety" means. Fascinating to feel the full scope of what the simple choices for survival and safety led to within mankind as a whole. To see us then and to know us now is fascinating to me.

DR: Amazing. To witness carrying forward some of this energy and consciousness?

DS: To witness the consciousness lose its strength, to witness judgment and choices erode the clarity, to lose the remembrance of their beginning. We do not make light of it. We are fully aware of how the humans have become, and are sorrowful to witness it.

But in the beginnings of our experiment, it was as fascinating to us to watch the erosion of that higher consciousness as it was for you to discover that you could split an atom. We did not know such could be done. We did not know such could happen.

And in this, I can feel the higher levels of CREATION itself growing in directions it had never grown before either. If I put this in religious terms, I would say, "God did not know this could happen." It just feels like the erosion of the consciousness wasn't anticipated and had never been witnessed before.

#4 Recording 2:20 *Beliefs of Adam and Eve*

DR: Did Adam and Eve teach a spiritual belief system to their offspring and others?

DS: It does not feel as if a belief system was taught. It feels as if a way of life was taught; a respect was taught; a consideration, a compassion was lived and through living, taught. So, it doesn't feel like there was a catechism class. It feels like there was an approach; the way the life unfolded. And then chastisement when that behaviour was countered, when there was disrespect, when there were reactions and overreactions. That is, when teaching took place. But for the most part we would say their teaching was by the doing, by the living of it.

As that occurred, we are going to say that the next generation, two generations down, their children, their grandchildren started to see it as a way of living, and then it began to manifest as a teaching. But initially, it was a way of being, not a teaching.

#4 Recording 9:40 *Adam Lineage*

DR: Is the lineage from Adam on down listed in the Bible accurate?

DS: For the most part we would say yes. There was a camaraderie in the tribes and strong memory and storytelling in the tribes and so the lineage was able to be followed. There are one or two errors in it, but not worth being concerned about, so our answer to you is yes.

DR: So, there was a spiritual tradition that began about two generations after Adam and is that a tradition that persisted throughout the progeny?

DS: There is a problem with your label being "spiritual tradition".

We brought consciousness to the beings we created to bring more awareness to the planet. But consciousness dictated a behaviour. It only evolved into a teaching when the behaviour was no longer natural, when there were things that disrupted the behaviour.

There was no need for a spiritual teaching in the beginning. It was a conscious way of being.

What was lived in the beginning was taught only after misbehaviour occurred. Only after selfishness and hoarding and competition started was a spiritual teaching needed. Prior to that, it was the way to live, the way to be. It did not need to be taught; it was the way of being.

But once the separations occurred, and the tectonic plates moved; once people were more isolated and the behaviour changed, that's when memory turned the way it used to be into a teaching.

In this answer about teachings versus consciousness, I feel the difference. Teachings are applied and make demands of behaviour. Whereas the behavior that consciousness dictated in the beginning feels very different. It feels less efforted, more natural, more authentic and the consciousness is simply being walked in living, not being applied to living.

#9 Recording 44:47 *Average Lifespan*

DS: What would the average lifespan have been in those generations?

DS: 180 to 200 years. Then as you cross the 32nd generation, it is closer to 100 to 150. And then when you come to the Abraham times, it is more like 100.

There is a need to clarify that this is not every person. Those of the faith, those of the leadership of the tribe, those that were led by the guidance of their faith, lived longer. They were kept safer, they were fed better, they were kept free of sickness and away from illness. They were preserved, *that is not the right word, but it is the word I have to use.* And so it was not the average life of the average man. It was the life of the leaders.

#2 Recording 28:44 *Offspring*

DR: Adam and Eve were able to procreate and the Bible lists Cain and Abel and later Seth. But were there other offspring before or after those three named in the Bible?

DS: We are seeing eight offspring, and at the time that the continental shelves shifted, they went in various directions.

When I ask if they procreated with their siblings, I am told no.

There were eight siblings when the continents shifted. They went in twos, different directions. They did not procreate together.

When I ask if they procreated with the humanoids, I am told once or twice only. When I ask if there were more creations made, I am told no. And so, I cannot see at this point how procreation occurred.

DR: Of these eight offspring of Adam and Eve, were some before Cain and Abel?

DS: The first offspring was female; second offspring was male; and so one for sure was before Cain. And it feels as if there was another female, either before Abel or after.

DS: It does not feel like there were an equal number of male and females. There were more males. But it was as if the Bible left out the females. We can see in this the seeds of judgment. These seeds of judgment weren't present in Adam and Eve or the offspring. But in the telling of their story, there are the seeds of judgment. The stories did not represent the equality that was present.

I am with the offspring and sensing the answer to this question. Then, as we get closer to the story of the Bible, I can sense the presence of judgment being attached to the story. I feel the distinct difference between the reality I am standing in, and the Bible stories later being written. They are two, quite distinct feelings and viewpoints. I can truly feel, the equality that was present with Adam and Eve. It was very real. True Equality. Then in sensing that, it brings complete clarity to me of the "seeds of judgment" that are in the Bible stories. It is fascinating to me to witness the beginning of judgment at this time. The sense of true equality is light and clear, open, whereas the sense of the Bible stories has contraction, heaviness, and density within the "seeds" of judgment.

Chapter Five

LEAVING EDEN

#9 Recording 34:02 *Freeing Adam and Eve to Grow*

DS: As we realized the Earth was settling, we understood that those of the Earth were settling as well.

That another level of evolution was occurring though we did not call it evolution in our discovery of it, but we could feel that those that were of the Earth were also changing with the Earth. And that if we wanted the Adam and the Eve to change with the Earth, they had to be free to the Earth, so they could change with her.

At this stage we did not identify it as evolution, but only as change. And if we had kept the Adam and the Eve in the

Eden, they would not have changed with the Earth. So as we started to realize that the Earth as a being, was growing and changing, and with her all that was of the Earth wanted to follow her, we needed to free the Adam and the Eve so that they could follow. And so the breaking of the wall, the first wall of Eden, was taken into our consideration. We decided that it was time to let the Adam and the Eve become of the Earth and follow change as all the creations of the Earth did. And so they were freed from what we call our environment of Eden and we allowed then Eden to be destroyed. They then began to evolve as other creatures did.

I see and feel the full effect of the Earth changes on the experiment of Eden. I can again feel the dedication of the Counsel to their experiment. There is present a true determination within the Counsel, that Adam and Eve "be" as the Earth is. There is a sense of scientific realization that for Adam and Eve to be of the Earth now, they must be with the Earth in her developing and changing time. I can sense that this is a change in the plan for their experiment, but their dedication to the purpose of the experiment, easily supersedes their plans. Truly, I am aware of the Counsel and what their experiment of Adam and Eve is all about.

And so the sense we have is that the Counsel **freed** Adam and Eve to become the creatures of the Earth that they wanted them to be. As if the Eden gave us the opportunity to still work with the consciousness and to create within them what we hoped they would bring to the planet. But at one point we realized that they must be of the planet and no longer of us or else they would be left behind in the changes of the planet.

Next, the Counsel moves my focus to them and the word "freed" is of great importance. I can feel that the Counsel "decided" to free

Adam and Eve and to really let go of their experiment at this time. I can feel the truth of their realization and the importance of them letting Adam and Eve now go and "be" of the Earth. I can sense that this is a great turning point in the experiment, and I can feel the expanding impact of "freeing" Adam and Eve to the Earth's changes.

#9 Recording 54:08 *Timelessness, Long Lives*

DS: They were still learning of the Earth, witnessing the Earth, exploring the Earth, but still separate from the Earth even though Eden did not keep them separate. There was fear. There was discomfort, and there was some hiding from some savagery. They had an ability to hide themselves and to hide their home, their place. It was the third generation from Adam that started to lose those abilities that they had learned in Eden, to hide themselves, to make things invisible, to hold timelessness. And it is in the latter generations, where we are seeing that the leaders are so much older. The leaders held a memory of that timeless ability. And so different leaders could live longer lives, because they knew of timelessness. They would not call it such. It was something that was passed down, something that was taught from elder to elder. And so, the ones like Moses and Abraham, without knowing it, knew how to live without time. They wouldn't see it that way. They would just be seen as strong, older, long-lasting, by the grace of God. But in actuality, they held some of the timeless beliefs in the actual cells of their body, and so it was many, many, many generations before timelessness was lost in mankind. And there are still those on your planet, in the tribes that live in the simplicity of life, that still know of timelessness and can have years pass by and still only celebrate one birthday every five years, or every twelve years as if time is not known.

#3 Recording 34:08 *Recreating Eden*

DR: After the Eden, the walls were taken down, the plates were moving, and Adam and Eve and their progeny left or moved. Did they try to create a second Eden?

DS: No. They recognized what was lost. They did not know how it had been lost. They recognized elements that they needed, and so was born the concept of tribe, of village, of cohabitating together. But the miraculousness of the original Eden, they had lost that awareness and magic, and could not recreate it.

Different circles, different villages, different children of Adam and Eve tried in different ways. The result of which is the dynamic uniqueness of the tribes of your planet. Each creating from their own awareness and their own memories what they could. But their creative ability was limited. We did not interfere.

There was talk of assisting, but when we watched them think, come together, design, we decided to leave it. And their natural instinct of the Earth seemed to take over and they found a way to feed, to grow food, to interact with the surroundings, and to protect themselves from the surroundings.

And in that growth, there were weaknesses. There was the emergence of cooperation but also competition. Very subtle, very small, but the seeds were planted, and we did not want to interfere with that which was happening. We had recognized EVOLUTION by this point and did not want to intercede or interfere with what was evolving. We did not know where it would take you. But we made a decision not to interfere with it.

When the question about any attempt to re-create Eden is asked, the answer is clear and concise. It has a "business" like attitude to it. The Counsel is truly clear in what their purpose was, and would not step in. As I can see what the Counsel is saying, I see the "evolution" taking place. Fascinating to actually "see" evolution taking place. To see ideas materialize; to see cooperation and then some competition grow.

The aliveness of life on so many levels is fascinating. Beliefs are alive. Ideas are alive. Cooperation is alive and growing. Competition is born and becomes alive. The process of EVOLUTION, beyond the physical realm, is amazing!

There is some sadness in the Counsel at where it took us. *But sadness is not even the right word, perhaps regret, that feels too strong. There is an acknowledgement in the Counsel that when they allowed evolution to re-create their own Edens, it gave birth to some things that they …regret … is not the right word, that they're sorry?*

Had they interfered, perhaps that might not have been, that might not have come about.

That little bit of competition, that little bit of fear, that little bit of selfishness…they truly did not recognize what that would evolve into. At the moment there was this, "Let's let them be who they are".

DR: The competition, was this between the different groups or tribes, or between individuals… or both?

DS: It began first with the hungers. Hunger needed to be answered. And so, competition and cooperation came out of hunger. Cooperation came first; competition came later. It came out of the needs: hunger, protection, survival. It came out of the survival needs.

It evolved. EVOLUTION is incredibly powerful on the Earth. We had not witnessed it this way elsewhere, and the EVOLUTION and its power amazed us. And because we did not, had not witnessed it before and did not truly understand it, we would not interfere with it.

The power of EVOLUTION, I can feel it expanding as if it is of life itself. It is truly amazing. It is a force of its own. I have never experienced the feeling of such a force and its naturalness, to change and grow.

DR: How many different groups were there initially that split off when the first Eden fell?

DS: Seven. The eighth came from the seventh, as if the seventh gave birth to that which became the eighth. The seventh was the first one to expand. The seventh feels to be more in the northern hemisphere, closer to the colder places, the colder weathers.

When we perceive them, we see seven circles, and we feel as if we are just above the equator. And it crosses the equator. There is one that just crosses the equator, that's two. There is one that comes back up across the equator, that's three. Four and five are close by, six is further north, seven is further north. And eight came from seven, so eight came much later, a generation later.

DR: But in this time were the continents much different than they are today?

DS: Yes. This was when the plates were just splitting and in some instances the splitting of the plates isolated the circles, isolated the tribes. It is as if there was a calling; there was an inkling in the consciousness of places that were more dangerous than others. And so, the tribes, the children, they moved, and then the tribes were created in the effort to re-create Eden.

DR: Were the dangers primarily the large animals?

DS: The dangers were all natural. They were of the Earth, of her movement, volcanic, oceans, disruptions in the weathers. The animals? We want to say no to that. *Take me there, please. Show me.* The dangers from the animals evolved. When the hungers got so strong, when the animals started to be sacrificed, that's when the animals became dangerous. Because the consciousness shifted. The conscious connection between animal and man shifted. The hungers became more important than the animals. And there was hoarding, and that is when the animals became dangerous. Initially, the animals were not dangerous. The animals hunted; the humans hunted; there was a harmony.

But when the hungers and the fears of the hungers and the fears of the weather, and the fears of that which they could not control in the evolution of the planet fed the hungers; the hungers then caused man to be very selfish and disconnect from the consciousness of the animals. They did not want to feel the consciousness of that which they destroy or ate, had to kill more of.

Previously there was a balance. But with the weather shifts, with the tectonic plate shifting, stores of food were needed.

And that's when the balances between human and animals shifted. And the animals became aggressive, protective of their own kind and saw man as dangerous.

I am actually witnessing and can sense the conscious relationship between the humans and the animals and witness it shift into the more selfish need to hoard the food. I feel the humans withdraw from their feeling connection to the animals and become more distanced from the animals' consciousness. I feel humans separate from them. It is fascinating to witness.

DR: In Eden, Adam and Eve and their offspring were provided with food or at that point they really didn't need much sustenance because of their nature.

DS: They did eat, but there was a harmony. They took the weaker of the herd. They were grateful to the animals for fair hunting. As the wolves hunt the rabbits, they catch the weak ones, they catch the young ones. Humans were the same and there was a respect. They took what they needed, and nothing more, just as the animals did.

So, there was an understanding of survival that was between humans and the animals. But then when the weathers changed and the planet changed and stores of food were needed, the animals did not understand this, because the animals sacrificed themselves. What we mean by this is they did not have the consciousness to prepare for the release. They did not have the inklings or the callings telling them to prepare. And so, when they lived, they lived, and if they were cold in the winter, they starved. If they were in the wrong place when things shifted, they died. There was more acceptance of the natural course of events.

Humans, when they started to get inklings and understand… they weren't trying to prevent the evolution, they were trying to stay alive during it. The animals never acquired that need. Their survival instinct was much more immediate. They did not have the ability to perceive what was coming. They could run from the tsunamis, they could run from the volcano, but they did not have the precognition as the humans started to receive, that the volcano was coming or that the tsunami was coming.

And so, the animals misunderstood and lost connection in the harmony, lost harmony with the humans. When the humans needed to store food, when the humans needed to take more than what was needed for the moment; that is what destroyed that harmony with the animals, and the hunt became something else. It became a competition. Who was braver, who was stronger, who would dominate? The hunt itself, for the stores of food, for the floodings, for the volcanoes, for the cold times, that very survival evolved on its own.

And the animals had inklings of where not to be; the mothers of the herd would take the herd new directions without knowing why. But they weren't preparing for it the way the humans were. The humans had precognition and could prepare for it which came from the consciousness that we gave them.

DR: During this time period what kinds of animals were present? Were they similar to the mammals of today or were they more ancient like the dinosaurs?

DS: Generally, we would say they were larger, similar to today but larger, and there were animals that are present with you today that were not present then. They were stronger, faster, larger. There were fewer species. Said another way... EVOLUTION created five kinds of lions or five kinds of cats. Initially there was one. There was one of this and one of that, and then that EVOLUTION created the varieties. There weren't the varieties that you have now. That came out of EVOLUTION. There weren't two kinds of horses, there weren't twelve kinds of snakes.

In these explanations about the animals, I see the Earth as it was. I am viewing the Earth, her changes, and the animals. At the same time, I can feel/sense the change in attitude, the difference in consciousness between animals and humans. I can literally feel the humans become less reactive, less animalistic and feel the consciousness that the Counsel embedded here, begin to grow.

That consciousness enabled the humans to prepare for the Earth changes. I am also witnessing the animals and where they are not prepared, where they are caught off guard by events. I sense "fight or flight" but not preparation in the animals. It seems to accentuate the preparedness to me, in the humans.

#9 Recording 1:00:48 *Gifts of Eden*

DS: I am now perceiving that these higher consciousness introductions were what we are now calling the Gifts of Eden: the timeless awareness, the memories, the simplistic, the depth of faith, the depth of knowledge, and the dedication. These were not disciplines. These were the Gifts of Eden. And different families were stronger in different gifts.

And again, that is why the timing is completely off. I cannot count it. We can count it in generations, but you still cannot add a hundred and two hundred years for every generation, because for the first five generations there are thousands of years. And then as the tribes spread, the tribe that had timelessness, their timing would be very different. Every tribe had timelessness, but they had different strengths of it.

Then, as the world evolved, the Gifts of Eden started to fade. It was one of the reasons the writings occurred, so that we could remember the Gifts of Eden and know that they were still possible. They weren't just miracles. They were teachings. They were consciousness. It was awareness. That is what the Counsel hoped would stay in the Earth and stay in the humans, and watched EVOLUTION undo it.

As I am allowed to share with the Counsel, their witness to the fading of the Gifts of Eden, I am left with a deep understanding of this and with a great hope for our future. I am left feeling hopeful because in these understanding that the Gifts of Eden are within us, perhaps they can be accessible again. Also, the integrity of the Counsel is reinforced to me when I am with them as they witness EVOLUTION undo the Gifts of Eden and yet still allow it to happen.

#2 Recording 38:11 *Judgment*

DR: The judgment is from where to where? Who is judging whose decisions?

DS: The judgment begins when the walls of Eden come down, and the protections are gone. So, judgment must be made as to where the water is. The season, where to be. Now that they know the plates can move, where is safe and where is unsafe. Now that the walls are gone, the relationship with the animals also changes. The provision of food is now their own responsibility. And then as they attack the animals, the animals attack them. And so, all this interaction shifted because the Eden had provided everything, and when the Eden walls left, it wasn't just protection; all the provision was gone as well.

And there was truly the beginning of what your language would say "living off the land". At first it was done with great ceremony and permission. Animals were involved in their sacrifice. Consciousness spoke to consciousness. But then as weather and tectonic plates, and the planet itself, shifted, then survival was threatened, and we watched the consciousness degrade. We watched judgment get stronger; survival instinct and fear grow. Such was not ever witnessed before, and it was unanticipated.

#9 Recording 56:35 *Timelessness, Difficulty with Timing Events*

DS: *And so as I stand among them, trying to find timing for you, it's hard because there is timelessness here. And then there is a time, when time seems to invade and then they remember how to stop time from invading, and they move back to being timeless. And they procreate, but in a very slow timeless fashion.* And so we are suggesting for your guidance and counsel that perhaps this is where the timing is all off.

Because as I sit with Adam and Eve outside of Eden, there is a timelessness, like a field around them that keeps that which is time on the Earth away from them. It seems as if they are still waiting for the moment where they are to align to the time of Earth, enjoying the time of Earth.

But it is not a knowledge. It's that timelessness is holding, so that the structure of the Eden is gone, but some of the Gifts of

Eden stay with them. That is how they became known to the storytellers, "the Gifts of Eden".

Timelessness was one of the Gifts of Eden as was birth to older women. Memory, shared memory is also one of the Gifts of Eden. It was not so hard for a storyteller to learn the stories. Memory was another Gift of Eden. It is why there were storytellers in one line of family, generation after generation, because that family line had managed to hold the Gift of Eden which was memory. And they perceived it as that. When the storyteller elder taught the storyteller younger, he was really just wakening, reminding the younger that he knew. It was how the truth was held. But then as they moved further and further from the Gift of Eden, called memory, the embellishments began.

And so in the procreation from Adam, it is very difficult to give you years. Because even if we give you generations, which makes the Counsel happy, I now see that perhaps the first ten generations after Eden could easily have been ten or twenty or thirty thousand years, because each generation was still in its timeless place.

The timelessness started to fade, in the sixth generation, the fifth generation. *I'm not sure, because it faded; it did not stop. **It evolved.*** There was timelessness for a period of so many years and then there was time. Time invaded, and then timeless took over again, and time did not affect. Then time invaded. Timelessness was a fading strong wall that faded in its strength and then rejuvenated in its strength and then faded. And so time is just impossible to put to it.

The timelessness was so strong until at least the fifth generation after Eden, after Adam, maybe even as far as the eighth, because then we see the generations having moved around the planet and each had their own Gift of Eden. Different generations had different Gifts of Eden, and different strengths to those gifts. Some were stronger in the memory, some were stronger in the timelessness, and some were stronger in the simplistic, in the faith.

As we explore the end of Eden with this question of time, I find that they are still in timelessness and so I struggle to put time language into this answer. As before, we then switch to following generations and things are clearer with that method. But still as I sense them leaving Eden and entering the Earth, they still hold an aura of timelessness. They are still very different from their surroundings on Earth. As I struggled to explain what I am sensing I realize that the timelessness is evolving and as those of Eden become more and more "of Earth" they lose timeless and enter time. This is another example of how the higher consciousness that the Counsel inserted here is affected by Earth's nature to evolve. The loss of timelessness is no sin, no punishment; it is simply EVOLUTION.

Interesting, the phrase "of the Earth but not from the Earth" comes to me. In these first moments of leaving Eden and inhabiting Earth, they are just that. On Earth but not yet of the Earth in the sense of aging and time. Fascinating to see and even more fascinating to feel the timelessness of them in their living as humans and how that is passed down through the generations. I can actually see the "wise ones" who can live longer lives but do not think anything of it but that it is miraculous and from the Grace of God. And then to witness in small pockets of the Earth now, simple tribal beings who still have this timeless within them and still do not know or recognize it as such. Fascinating to see our Earth and mankind from this perspective.

#8 Recording 47:58 *The Story of Cain and Abel*

DR: Can you explain the Cain and Abel story and what happened there?

DS: The first thing we have to say is it was the birth of independence.

There was some retaliation to the strictness of Adam and Eve, to the strictness of the laws of Eden, or the perceived laws of Eden. There were no laws given to Eden, but there was a perception of needing to live in gratitude, needing to be respectful of all that was alive in Eden.

The story of Cain and Abel is the first disagreement, independence rising, a sense of self wanting something that the others did not have. It was the first conflict where both wanted to be right, but one needed to be wrong. It was the first realization that someone could want something that was not of the way to be. It was the first independent, perhaps called *selfish act*. Cain was the one who wanted something else, and Abel wanted it to stay as it had always been.

DR: Was there an actual killing or murder of Abel by Cain?

DS: Yes, because this was the birth of one being right and one being wrong. It was the first moment that disturbed the peace of sameness. It was the first birth of difference, and it was primal within Cain. It was overwhelming and dominating. When this first murder occurred and Cain woke to what he had done, there was deep shame and great fear. It was the first conflict that resulted in death. It was the first time one needed to triumph over the other. It again was a turning point in the dynamics of the developing inner self, the independent thinking, the independent desire.

But it does feel as if there was such shame within Cain that he softened his desires greatly, and managed his desires greatly as if he came to a pinnacle of something he did not ever want to experience again. He did not walk away the winner. He walked away the loser. And the shock of Abel's death also diminished the growth of the differences of desire, in something different, of asking for more.

DR: Was he forgiven by his parents, and did he go into exile?

DS: He was not forgiven. He was forgiven later, but he would never know it. For Adam and Eve needed to find the forgiveness, to understand what had occurred, and to see what was changing and how to administer it, how to manage it.

Cain left in shame. He, in shame and shock, left of his own accord. And was followed by his wife, his woman, a friend. There was Cain, another man, another woman, maybe a child that left. And he left in fear and in shame.

It actually changed him to be more like Adam again. He had been changing and becoming less like Adam, and there had been a deliberateness to it, a fight within himself not to copy his father. And it feels like this event caused him to respect his father more and to curtail and manage that part of him that wanted to be different. And he was rather strict with his children after this. So, he did not leave this a winner. He left this woken to a danger that was growing within him. And he saw it that way and managed it.

It made a change in the dynamics that actually supported the original beliefs of Adam and Eve in Eden, and followed Cain in his line, because he did not leave this a winner. He wanted to be sure that no one ever felt what he felt, that none of his children ever came to that point.

And so the dynamic of how personal choice was managed changed with Adam and Eve, and it changed with Cain and those that followed Cain. Abel's death had awoken an awareness in Adam and Cain that sameness was changing, and it had to be managed; that if the change wasn't managed, the change wasn't allowed in some way, it would be dangerous. It could not be just suppressed.

Chapter Six

COUNSEL'S WORDS

#2 Recording 23:57 *CREATION and the Counsel*

I feel this Counsel in an experiment on the Earth, and CREATION using the Counsel to evolve so much more than another life form. It was a science experiment on the Earth by a species. **But also,** CREATION's forces were using inspired ideas of the Counsel to experiment so much further than they realized. It feels as if there is a CREATION, Creator, God element, using the Counsel. This Counsel is far more evolved than the humans, but still beings, experimenting, but their inspiration is where it feels as if CREATION is using science to create.

#2 Recording 39:45 *How the Counsel Views Earth Events*

DR: So how does the Counsel watch and see what is happening? How do they perceive the changes on Earth, the beings starting to evolve?

DS: There are dimensions in the higher realms. Our timing is different. And so, what would occur in a week would be moments or minutes for us. We have not the time structure that you have. And so, we are witnessing through our presence, but we are…invisible, *but that's not the right word*…watching, *but that's not the right word*…participating, *but it's not the right word*.

It's like there is this dimensional viewing and so they are very able to witness the evolution on the Earth, because they have not time where they are. And so, what are days and weeks and months and years, and millennia is very different for them. And so, it is like watching, I want to say, a screen, but it's not, because there is contact. They are present with the watching. They are with the watching. So, it is not as removed as a screen would make it sound. But it is removed dimensionally, because they have no structure of time. And so, because time is on the Earth, time allows them to witness and watch and move through time to perceive. The way you would take a tape and go forward and back in the recording.

But we have no recording, we are present and because we have no time we can move through your time and be present at this and present at that moment in your time.

DR: Are they able to see possible, probable future events as well?

DS: *When this question is asked there is a sadness in the Counsel. They have and still uphold witnessing and can hypothesize the future of mankind.*

Again, the EVOLUTION has surprised us, and so there isn't a certain future for the humans. There are possibilities, and we can see those possibilities, but are waiting to see what possibilities will manifest. There is so much choice on the Earth now that the possibilities lead different people in different directions. We do not mean to imply that there are a dozen different Earths. That is not our truth. But to generalize the direction of your planet has to wait, because it is the union of similar choices.

There is a harmony when a group of you make similar choices and direct the energy in a similar fashion. And that harmony then directs the Earth herself. And there are several possible directions, because choice is so alive... *they like that word...* ALIVE on the planet. One of the most fascinating aspects of the experiment is the choice. And we are very aware that the birth of choice came from our choosing to remove the walls of Eden, to remove the protections and the provisions, and let, to use your phrase, "let Nature take its course".

#2 Recording 55:37 *Consciousness versus Nature*

DS: And so that was not anticipated when we made humans of the Earth. We didn't anticipate that the higher consciousness we gave them would at times compete with the evolutionary nature. Said another way, the tadpole could decide it didn't want to lose its tail and it would fight its own evolution.

Humans sometimes fight their own evolution.

We find that fascinating. We find that sad, and we are sorry we did not anticipate it.

Simultaneously to this conversation with the Counsel, I can sense/feel CREATION itself, and CREATION is in joy; CREATION knew what the Counsel did not.

As this is spoken, I can sense and see how the "evolutionary nature" of the Earth changed mankind. I can feel/see how it brings us to this state of chaos now, in 2021. I have a sense of the overall impact. It is almost overwhelming to me, personally, to witness in a flash how this evolutionary nature of the Earth herself, affects and changes humans and leads us to where we are now. It is a fascinating few seconds, as the whole of the evolution of humans flashes before me.

DR: It's becoming clearer now. Cells from the Earth which had a natural inclination to evolve, were, in part, used to create the humans, Adam's and Eve's bodies, which then imparted evolutionary drive in the humans that they created.

DS: And then as the humans naturally evolved the higher consciousness, there was… *disharmony is too strong of a word*… sometimes conflict between the natural evolution of the human and the consciousness decisions.

When the humans allow their consciousness to trust their evolution, it's beautiful to watch. But when they try to control it, it is interference, and you are living some of those results.

As Earth evolved, as that EVOLUTION started, there was a sense of contributing further. The belief systems were open to impact, to contribute. And so, it was through the belief systems that we (the Counsel) knew we could further contribute. And those you have named are part of the belief system and we used that belief system to contribute further. There was a fascination at the time to watch a belief system be born and grow.

It began as a blaming: blaming the sun for the darkness, blaming the weather for the starvation or the problems of the floodings. It began as a blaming. But it was fascinating to watch it shift and change. And so, we saw how alive the belief system was and saw that was a place we could contribute.

I can feel that as the Counsel witnessed the development of our belief systems, there appeared another opportunity for impacting our development. It is fascinating to see our belief system actually as an entity that is alive. I could see our beliefs grow and change and with each change, I am witnessing the "aliveness" of our beliefs.

As the Counsel speaks directly through me, at one point, I am within the understanding of "blaming" and can sense where that would lead. In my blended state with the Counsel I can share in what and when they first witness blaming and then, without detail, I can sense where this "blaming" leads, how this leads humans to where we are now. I perceive it like a timeline of belief system growth. I perceive no details, but a sense of the power of beliefs and their growth is very strong.

#3 Recording 49:21 *Evolution of Consciousness*

DR: When Adam and Eve were created, with them came a new energy that raised the consciousness of the planet. How did that energy persist, especially if it got diminished in their offspring? How did that energy persist on the planet?

DS: It did not initially increase the consciousness of the planet, itself. The Earthen Mother absorbed the consciousness of the humans we created and welcomed them into the network of nature. The consciousness evolved with the needs. And so, the consciousness was less at its inception then it was by the time of the first generation.

The mother Earth allowed the consciousness as we intended it to weave in, the humans to be part of the weave. To be recognized by nature as part of nature because they were created from the nature of the planet. The consciousness allowed them as the individual being to evolve. But nature directed that evolution.

I feel the acceptance by the Earth of what the Counsel has added to the Earth. I am within the consciousness of the planet and can feel this answer that the Counsel offers. It brings a whole new definition to the idea "we are all connected". I can feel Earth and Earthen Mother, I can feel Nature, I feel the weaving. In this moment, I know that it is true – everything is connected!

That is where we (the Counsel) lost understanding. We thought the consciousness would evolve nature, but nature evolved the consciousness.

Because the human was made up of the nature of the Earth, they evolved as the Earth evolved. They evolved as everything evolves on Earth. And so, the consciousness itself was included in the evolution. And so, there were distortions in the consciousness and those distortions came from its evolution being directed by the natures.

Your Earth evolves out of nature, evolves out of need. As your brain evolves, and acquires knowledge, tastes, varied experiences, it creates new needs that are not natural needs. The needs that have evolved, evolved out of the consciousness' evolution.

The animals did not evolve to have more and more needs, to have more and more variety, because they were part of the nature.

We introduced something to the planet that was not of the planet, wove it into the consciousness of the planet. And so, the evolutionary consciousness of the planet evolved through the consciousness we implanted. And it created a mind; it created knowledge; it created more experiences, as we wished it to. But out of that also came an evolution of more need, an importance of need, a selfishness of need, an isolation and need.

The evolution of need combined with a consciousness created an entire evolution of need that was not anticipated. So, the needs of your humans as you are now are not survival needs. They are not food; they are twelve kinds of food. They are not lodgings; they are larger lodgings. They are twelve acres of lodgings. They are not vehicles; they are twelve vehicles. The needs evolved and the consciousness fed the evolution of the needs. And so that which is beyond your immediate needs is how the consciousness (which we implanted) evolved.

DR: So, initially, the higher consciousness that came to Earth with the creation of Adam and Eve was absorbed by the planet, by the nature?

DS: When we say absorbed, we mean that the consciousness did not go into the animals or into the planet. It's like there were connections, weavings where, even though Adam and Eve and their consciousness were not born on the planet, they felt like they were born on the planet.

If the planetary space was a blanket of multi-coloured threads, we wove in a new colour of thread, and it was accepted into the blanket. It didn't change the other colours, but it harmonized with the other colours, initially. And as it harmonized with the other colours, these weaves wove into the planet itself.

There was respect of the animals. There was recognition of the creatures. There was respect of the nature. And then all of that was allowed to weave in with them (Adam and Eve). But when those original weavings connected to the consciousness, the consciousness evolved. We did not expect the consciousness to change as it did. We didn't know consciousness would evolve. And when consciousness evolved, it evolved through the needs. And so, the needs multiplied. And then as the needs multiplied, some of the other qualities of the humans were born. Competition, power, selfishness. These came out of needs.

But it was the evolution of consciousness that gave birth to those needs. It evolved the way all of the planet evolved, which is from need. Such as the creation of fangs, the creation of tongues, the creation of tails, they evolve out of need. The consciousness evolved out of need. But then it created more needs. And the consciousness evolved in ways we had never anticipated.

I am sensing how the consciousness was brought to the planet by the Counsel, was then taken over by the nature of EVOLUTION and then instead of consciousness affecting nature, it was nature that affected consciousness. The result was that our consciousness evolved in the natural way of the planet, through the needs.

I can watch the evolution and how it kept expanding and expanding. I can feel Counsel witnessing and allowing the evolution to continue. I see how Adam and Eve were "woven" into the Earth and how they affected all that the Earth was. It is an enormous expansion as I watch it grow and change. It is like watching a plant grow in an accelerated mode.

I see how Adam and Eve are "woven" into the Earth. I see and feel the nature of evolution accept Adam and Eve and then see how that same accepting evolution, then works through Adam and Eve to evolve what they are in the consciousness. It is like watching creation work. It is steady and consistent.

Whatever is introduced to the Earth and her evolution then becomes able to evolve and so the "needs" of humans also evolved. The creativity, the inventiveness of the humans, continued to evolve as nature on the Earth intended everything of the Earth, to evolve. And with our creative consciousness, our needs evolved beyond the simple survival needs.

#3 Recording 56:33 *Solution for Man?*

DR: Is there a solution for mankind?

DS: The needs rule the consciousness now. The consciousness wants to become stronger and not a victim of the needs.

Is there a solution?

<u>We (the Counsel) are no longer part of the solution.</u> We accept,

in the science of it all, that the consciousness will evolve. And in the tribes where the consciousness will not evolve, mankind will become extinct. **And that will be its evolutionary end.**

Where the consciousness realizes extinction is near, the consciousness will evolve to its own solution. And its solution, as we perceive it, is tied to the relationship with needs. We don't see how, and if we saw we would not say, because it must come of its own evolution. It must come from yourselves. The needs have become more important than anything else. And the consciousness is ruled by the needs. When the consciousness is no longer ruled by the needs, you will save yourself. Where you do not, you will become extinct.

No one will save you because no one created this.

You evolved it. You have free will. You make choices based on your needs and that's where your power is.

Change comes through choice. We will not interfere with that. We have brought insight. We have brought light - that's not the word in your language, it does not mean what it means to us. We have brought understandings. We brighten realization. We brighten understanding. We open your eyes. We brighten you. But we can do no more than this.

When our consciousness touches yours, as it does through this one (meaning Donna), and with what it brings to you, we open your eyes, and we help you to see how important your choices are. And we help you to see what you are driven by, and what is more important than your choices.

And there are events that are being created on your planet to show you how you have prioritized your importance and how you have prioritized your needs, because you can choose to change that priority. You can choose to change that importance, but you must choose it. Where the tribes choose it, change will come. Where the tribes do not, extinction will come.

It is the same as the lion that did not have precognition of the volcano. He could feel the rumblings, he ran from it, but he didn't move his pack a month ahead the way the humans moved their pack.

Your consciousness can hear more; your consciousness knows more. When it is used to control for needs, it is misused. When it is used to expand consciousness, it is used in order. That is how we perceive you.

As the Counsel speaks about there being no one to save us, I can sense that the Counsel is offering a teaching. The Counsel speaks with scientific detachment, speaking what they have witnessed and the understandings they have come to in conclusion of the experiment. As if their part is over now and they now are witnesses to the experiment and its evolution.

I am left with the understanding of how important our choices are; how powerful our choices are. I can feel the Counsel waiting, watching as we the "experiment" now must take charge of our consciousness and make choices of how to use it. I can sense the simplicity of it which feels odd in our world so full of complications.

There is our appreciation for your curiosity. This is your consciousness breaking free of your needs. This is your consciousness asking for something more than the basic needs. This is your consciousness opening and we are grateful for the opportunity to be asked, to participate in your opening. We are present to help, but only as **YOU** ask of us.

The Counsel does not refuse to help. They refuse to interfere. I can feel they are willing to offer teaching, guidance when they are asked. But still they pull back to see how it is used. What each of us will do with this new perspective?

It is like the teacher in the movie <u>The Matrix</u>, saying, "I can only open the door, you must walk through it". It is ultimately up to each of us. There is such power in that realization, and I am very grateful to have felt it so deeply and completely. I am changed by these understandings.

Discussion

ADAM & EVE

#2 Recording 1:08:42 *CREATION versus EVOLUTION and Concept of Evil*

DS: As I was doing this, it was like there were two different connections. There was a connection to the Counsel, to those who created the human beings, and then there was this sense of God Creator – CREATION itself – raw potential creation, that was all about creating. And that CREATION inspired certain decisions in the Counsel. So, when there were times when the Counsel was confounded or surprised, I could feel a joy at the CREATION level, because CREATION wasn't surprised.

CREATION, *I am probably really oversimplifying this*, but it was like CREATION saw the universal joke. When CREATION inspired the Counsel to use the nature of Earth so that the beings would be harmonious, the joke was on them because there was this evolutionary gem in everything that they (the Counsel) didn't know about. And I could feel that there was such joy at CREATION's level, because this had allowed evolution to take place with the consciousness itself. Up until then, evolution was responsive to nature, to survival. We adapted, we grew fins or gills, or tails or teeth.

But when they embedded the evolutionary gem into the human beings, that then allowed consciousness to have an evolutionary experience. At times I can see the expanse of it, where it goes. I can just see the everything. And I could see how this led to consciousness trying to control nature. And nature trying to break free of consciousness. And this control we have which is selfish, "No. I'm going to build my tent here" or "I will stop the river," instead of building where the river will let them build. "I'm going to have my house on the north side, and we will just control the wind".

And I can see how we got into this mess. We fight EVOLUTION.

We fight EVOLUTION!

Because we don't trust EVOLUTION.

And for me personally, Evolution, God, Creator, God, Goddess, it's all the same thing. So, when I trust life, I'm trusting the evolution of it. And I could really see the myriad of problems that we have created because of the distrust of evolution. But

CREATION is joyful at it, because CREATION could not have created such imperfection.

Because in EVOLUTION there wouldn't be that kind of imperfection. It's only because, for lack of a better word, there was experimentation, intervention, that creation became flawed. Because EVOLUTION doesn't make mistakes. The tadpole doesn't keep the tail. The frog has no tail. The lion doesn't lose its teeth. The daffodil doesn't bloom in the snow.

EVOLUTION doesn't do that.

#3 Recording 1:02:14 *Listening, Avoiding Danger, Hoarding vs Simplifying*

DS: I have never believed from the age of 30 that this was supposed to be a hard place to live. I've never believed life was supposed to be difficult. I attributed it, in my youth, to religion, to God. As I entered metaphysics, I just had this feeling that if we would listen, we would know. And so, my focus has been, in my own personal journey, to listen better.

And now, it's so fascinating to me to know that we were able to listen much better initially, at our creation. We knew the plates were going to shift, and we knew when the volcanoes would erupt, and we knew when the winters would be worse. We knew when all of this was coming. And then, someone told the tribe, and the tribe would move. We would survive.

But then the listening was compromised. It became a gift and so only the medicine man or the chief, or the one person could listen.

Listening requires surrender and trust, because you can't surrender without trust. And so many humans won't listen; they won't surrender. And I see from what you (DR) asked here in Section One, that the listening came out of the needs. If the winters were going to be long, we had to have more than one stock of meat. And then, we started hoarding. We didn't know how much we were going to need, because the listening told us the cold was coming, but we couldn't hear well enough to know how long it would last. And so, fewer and fewer would listen. Then those that listened became the gifted ones.

And it's the listening that we have to develop; the consciousness that knew. But we've become selfish. We've become, you know, "Covid hits and a family of four has thirty packages of toilet paper." Like, excuse me, what's wrong with this picture! We've gotten distorted in our needs. I love what we have said here, "I never saw it so simply. It's the NEEDS. You simplify your needs; you simplify your life."

#3 Recording 1:06:06 *Consciousness and Needs*

DS: But to see it as being driven by the needs, that's fascinating. That's fascinating to me. It gives me food for thought in my own personal journey.

DR: But the fact that the consciousness and the needs evolved and grew. It wasn't just needs. But then needs shifted, and they grew... and they continue to grow. There is no limit!

DS: Consciousness is CREATION and there is no limit in CREATION. But there is a limit on the planet.

That's where the confusion is happening. That's why the

animals don't hoard. Animals hunt and eat. They don't hoard because they have this connection to the Earth that lets them realize the limitations of the Earth.

We are like an unlimited being in a limited space and we don't know what we are doing.

#3 Recording 1:07:53 *Distorted Needs*

DR: We have to corral them (our needs).

DS: We do. You see the Counsel brought to us this consciousness from an unlimited source and brought it to a limited planet. And I think, I don't want to use the word mistake, sorry, but if there's a mistake, that's it.

And there is something in the nature that when the natural evolution of the planet intersected with the consciousness of Adam, there was a distortion in the evolution of that consciousness. That's why the Counsel did not want us to see it as inserted, because if the consciousness did not come into the nature of the planet, then it has its own consciousness. It needed to be just another weave. But then the natural ability to evolve came into the consciousness, and then the consciousness evolved.

I might be oversimplifying it at this point, **but it feels to me that the consciousness of this planet is based on need.**

You get what you need. You take what you need, period. But when that need intersected with consciousness, the consciousness evolved, and the need evolved as well and, in its evolution, it's distorted.

116

DR: So, the higher consciousness that came with the creation of Adam and Eve persisted on its own?

DS: Yes.

DR: Like that was its own identity?

DS: Yes. But as needs evolved with it, the needs became as important as the consciousness, and then more important than the consciousness.

DR: Then, the higher consciousness wasn't passed on, inherited on an individual basis into the progeny, the biological progeny?

DS: It was, but it was 'infected' *for lack of a better word*. It was infected by the evolution of need at that point, so it wasn't pure consciousness any longer.

That's why our first attempts at connecting to pure consciousness were done with drugs, were done with teas, were done with isolations. Because it's like we had to take ourselves away from the needs to focus on the consciousness, and get clear in that consciousness.

I still have to meditate for 30 to 40 minutes every day that I work to get free of my mind, of my thoughts, of my needs. I still have to do that because I have to focus on just consciousness, because that consciousness is still there, but it's been overshadowed or overlayed or wallpapered. And you have to peel the layers back to get to the pure consciousness. That's how I perceive it. I peel things back to get to the pure consciousness.

#4 Recording 1:00:56 *Creating Adam and Eve*

DR: Do you get a sense at all with Adam and Eve that they were constructed on the planet? Was there some kind of place, building?

DS: This is interesting because I could see that. I don't think to say all that I see. But when they (the Counsel) were creating them, I could see this.

It was a silver, I want to say steel, room. There was glass. And first there was Adam. And there was a pillar of light that came out of the ceiling. There was a big tube coming out of the ceiling, maybe 18 inches in diameter. And there was two or three of them in the ceiling. And the first one is where Adam was. And the energy came out of that, and it connected to a small tube on the bottom. And that's where Adam was created.

And interesting, when they created Eve, Eve was in the tube next to him. And when I was watching it, it was like Adam wasn't completely finished when they decided to create Eve. So, he was still in the tube. He wasn't a walking, talking being. He was still in the tube, but he was formed. He was very white, very silver, with a sparkle to him almost.

DR: Was he (Adam) aware?

DS: No. He was there, but he wasn't awakened yet. It was like he wasn't complete. It was like watching something create a body, but hadn't woken it yet. He was still asleep in some way. And then Eve was created in the tube next to it. There was glass. They (the Counsel) were standing outside watching this happen.

And the glass was like three feet by three feet. And the bottom was all silver or steel, and there were frames of glass all the way around it, all three feet by three feet. And then the top was all silver. And the energy came through the top, through these tubes. And it was like Adam was held in the tube. But the tube was, I don't know, sixteen inches at the top and then it was just light and then maybe ten inches at the bottom. That's where the light anchored. It was like Adam was held in that tube of light and that's where he was created. And then, when he was almost complete, they decided to create Eve.

DR: (excited) But that's what I wanted to know before – I couldn't get the answer before when I asked about the creation of Adam and Eve.

DS: Next time ask me what else I see.

DR: Because that's what I was getting at, that they were actually physically, biologically, chemically created. But they did take elements of the Earth?

DS: Yes. They were made of the Earth. It was critical that they were made of the Earth. Now, I do not know how that manifested, but they were made of the Earth.

DR: But that creating happened on the Earth, in that building… was that thing you saw on the Earth?

DS: I don't know. I would assume, but I can't say I saw it on the Earth. I didn't see where it was. I just saw Adam being created.

DR: And there were other beings present, watching it?

DS: Yes, there was. I'd say four or six. They all had the same robes on. They were all the same height. They had facial structure, very light-colored, like not white-faced...

DR: They were in the building?

DS: Yes, they were right there inside, looking through the glass.

DR: OK, now we are getting there (light laughing).

DS: I couldn't see their faces. I was just aware of four standing just outside this structure. And I don't know how big it was. If this room I am in is eight by ten feet, it might have been ten by fifteen feet. But it was also like a tube, it was completely round, all glass.

DS: They had that lightness of skin, almost white, but almost translucent at the same time. And their robes were this really beautiful shade of brown – Indian red. And they were all the very same height and the very same stature. But there was life in them, they weren't creatures. They were alive. They weren't robots.

DR: So was it possible that creation took place on the Earth, and they were on the Earth doing this?

DS: Possible. Like I said, I can't see where this room is, so I don't know if it was in another dimension. I don't know if it was on the Earth. I don't know if it was on a ship. I didn't see where it was. I was just focused on the creation of Adam.

DR: This really puts it in the right light for me, because I'm a scientist. I'm a geneticist. I've done tissue culture, worked in a lab. So how did they do this?

DS: I want to say in my peripheral vision there is another level to my right that's up a little higher and that is where the controls are. There are two beings up there. And everything's silver. Everything looks like aluminum or stainless steel. I don't know what it is, but that's what it looks like.

It has that laboratory effect to it, but there is also a lot of glass like they want to be involved in watching. There is a lot of glass. But it's all energy. It's all coming out of the roof of this thing. It would almost look like a furnace pipe across the top that can feed into these. And there's two in front: Adam is here, and Eve is here. There is actually two more tubes that are not being used at the moment that I was watching Adam. There might be more on the other side.

#9 Recording 1:19:36 *Leaving Eden*

DS: What was called the Gifts of Eden, I have witnessed those in myself and others who do my work. I have experienced timelessness. I have teachers who are ageless, active, seventy-five as if they are forty. And so, it makes sense to me. But what is really fascinating, when I was trying to get years for you, I thought it was a resistance at first. But it was more like a misunderstanding, because the Counsel witnessed the Earth in terms of points marked by evolution, by change, by invention or innovation. And so it was like they were witnessing, and their attention was caught by a change, and then they are there, witnessing the change. And then it's like they were away and then brought back to pay attention again. In Eden, there was timelessness. I am going to say there wasn't hunger. There wasn't anything we know in Eden. It was a prefab environment.

And it was only when something happened that ... looked to me that a wall was broken. They wanted to keep <u>the</u> Adam and <u>the</u> Eve there longer, but if they didn't let them go when they did, they wouldn't be of the Earth anymore. It's almost like what they were made of, that made them of the Earth, was evolving so quickly that they would no longer be of the Earth. And so, it was almost against what they wanted, to free them when they did. But when they freed them, and that was the feeling, they (Adam and Eve) held these talents, these abilities. And so they stayed alone.

#9 Recording 1:21:58 *Procreation Insertion*

The last insertion to them before they were freed from Eden was procreation. And that didn't mean they procreated and had a kid nine months later. Everything was just so expanded in this timeless place, that I can see why when I ask them to show me the years, they couldn't. They couldn't because they do not look in terms of years, they look in terms of evolutionary points, changing points and then the gifts of Eden.

DR: What was the insertion?

DS: The insertion was like the last program they activated in the body. The need to procreate is the last program activated.

DR: So it was already present? They just activated it?

DS: Yes, it was not active, but present.

DR: They didn't put in like a DNA transformation?

DS: No. Well, I don't know, because as I perceive Eve, she has ovaries, but she wasn't menstruating. There wasn't that procreation need. So she had the equipment, but it wasn't turned on. Because the insertion felt like a program that turned on.

And it was the last thing done before they freed them from Eden. And even that, so that would have meant, I'm guessing here, that would have meant within months of leaving Eden, she would have started menstruating. But would she menstruate every thirty days? I don't know. Maybe every hundred years. I don't know, because they were still in timelessness. And they didn't have the need, the instinctive need for procreation. That was very dull at first. Fascinating.

#9 Recording 1:23:55 *Timeline for Eden*

DR: If we present this book and we say Eden was at a time when the Earth was still in flux, and then we try to relate that to generations from Adam and Eve to Abraham to Moses, it doesn't make sense. The Earth was in flux (meaning plates shifting) millions of years ago, real flux, tens of millions of years ago and the continents really shifted around. And so, if you reconcile that in some way, which was actually done pretty well in the answer, then this is no more believable than the Bible stories.

DS: Yes, I understand completely. Because what I saw when I went to that, it was like a realization in The Counsel that they had not been specific enough when they said that tectonic movement. And then, they showed the movement layers down, closer to the center of the Earth. And so, it's like the continents were formed and starting to stabilize, but there was still movement. It wasn't the Earth we are living in now. No, I understand the conflict completely.

#9 Recording 1:25:45 *Long Lifespans*

DR: So, the explanation brings things closer together, especially the unknown time of each generation. So, if there was fifty-some generations, Adam and Eve to Abraham and Sarah, and the timespan of each generation is variable and could be one or two thousand years, that kind of brings things a bit closer, much closer, and a lot more believable. So that was kind of the key to me. My questions are about physical things, and the Counsel wants to talk about evolutionary things, but for a book I feel I need to have some more clarity so that people will comprehend.

DS: No, I completely agree. Those first five generations, maybe eight, after Adam, could be thousands of years, because timelessness was really strong. Timelessness was really strong until at least the fifth generation, and then started to fade, but was still strong in the eighth generation. And then when the tribes separated, they all took their own understandings, the gifts we'll call them. And so, tribe A that went north. They might have held onto timelessness longer than tribe F that went south. Once they left Eden and were subject to the evolution of the Earth, the Gifts of Eden were subject to the evolution differently in different people.

#9 Recording 1:27:32 *Leaving Eden, Keeping Hidden*

DR: Did you see them actually leaving Eden?

DS: Yes, it was just the two of them. It was like they had

this ability to move to safer ground. They didn't go far, but it was like they had this ability to hide themselves. They knew how to manipulate energy in a way that they would choose who could see them and when they would be seen. But it wasn't protective. It was almost like they wanted to hold themselves against time, that they wanted to hold that timeless feeling. It's like Adam and Eve came out of Eden with a certain understanding, certain abilities that came from the understandings of what Eden was. And so, their pattern of living continued as it had been in Eden. Now they had to hunt; they had to fend for themselves more, but the idea of timeless and the idea of memories and all of that still stayed with them. So, they created their own environment because of what they were accustomed to.

They wouldn't have hunted the way the humanoids hunted, and they wouldn't have lived the way the humanoids lived. And they also still had that sense not to get involved, not to affect. Like if they saw a village of humanoids or a clan of humanoids, they wouldn't introduce themselves to them. They kept themselves separate. It was like they had this force field, though I can't call it that, which allowed them to not be seen.

THE MYTH OF EVIL - NO DEMON, NO DEVIL

In the story of Adam and Eve, the serpent makes its appearance as a deceiver. "*Now the serpent was the shrewdest of all the wild beasts that the LORD God had made. He said to the woman, "Did God really say: You shall not eat of any tree of the garden?"* (Genesis 3:1)

DR: So thus begins temptation, evil acts, and disobedience. According to the Bible, as a consequence, the serpent is punished by having to now crawl on its belly; the woman is punished by now having severe labour pains in childbirth; the man is punished by now having to toil for his food. The final punishment is that both humans are banished from Eden.

The myth of evil was embodied in a creature, the serpent. The serpent is a symbol for Satan, a fallen angel, and appears to have started with this myth. But when I asked about this story of the serpent and the origin of the myth of evil, surprisingly to me, the origin was not with the serpent in the Garden of Eden. It had an entirely different origin based on a misunderstanding, and then the myth of evil evolved further on its own.

#2 Recording 57:50 *Myth of Evil*

DR: I would like to go into the topic of the fall of man, the story of Eve, the apple, serpent and Satan, and that whole mythology.

DS: The story was written by the human who heard our story. It was the human's effort through judgment, looking for the origins of evil, the origins of conflict, the origins of selfishness. This (the serpent) was not the origin of these qualities.

There was a natural evolution taking place in the human, and it was beyond the control of the conscious mind. And the conscious mind became threatened, and fear was born. And when fear was born, these seemingly negative consequences, these seemingly labelled evil tendencies, came from that fear. It was merely, from our perspective, the fear of that which was beyond their choice.

The consciousness coming into the body was to experience choice, the evolution. But at times the evolution seemed to take over and leave no choice. For example, when the plates broke and the land moved, there was great danger. And the consciousness could not control this because it was the evolution of the planet herself.

Then, when the walls of Eden came down, and the humans hunted the animals, and did not connect to or respect the animals, the animals retaliated. The consciousness could not control this. It was an evolutionary thing in the animal itself, for its own survival. And so there were episodes from when the plates broke and the continents formed, and the Eden finished, but the evolution was taking directions that the consciousness could not control. And out of this was born a fear, and out of the fear was born ego, control, selfishness, director, a stronger mind.

As we said, we watched the degradation of the awareness of All into a controlling mindfulness. "How can we stop this?" (instead of "How do we run with this?") It was the loss of cooperation; it was the initiation of selfishness. It led to places we did not anticipate.

But the myth you ask about is a human hearing our story, at a time when there was a lot of selfish, damaging choices, trying to make sense of this. For when the humans of that era witnessed nature in nature's setting, away from the humans, there was cooperation; there was respect. Animals killed what they ate and killed no more. Young ones were protected. There was a kindness. There was something witnessed in the natural world that a human wanted to understand. And in his prayers and in his requests, we tried to answer him. But he was wanting a definition of where evil came from and his lack of understanding of what we are trying to explain to you, created the story of evil, created the story of selfish, created the story of weaker sex, stronger sex.

It is a story. He didn't want to hear our story; he wanted an answer to his question. When we gave him our story, he took that as an answer to his question.

We (the Counsel) were not clear. We did not realize how attached he was to his question of "Where did this bad, evil behaviour came from?" And so he took our story to be his answer, and he called it evil. We call it fear.

Note from Donna: Here the Counsel continues to speak about the evolution of the consciousness and their witness of that evolution. I can feel how the Counsel answered the questions of a man who was seeking to understand the origins of evil. I can see this man, in his prayer state, seeking this guidance. I can feel his sincerity and his true concern. He asks out of love, out of concern for his changing world. I can feel the Counsel being willing to help but then I can also see how this man does not have the capacity to arrive at the true understanding of what the Counsel presents to him.

With the beginning of fear, then selfishness, and control, I can feel the Counsel witness with interest and concern these developments. I can sense that their "answers" to this man of prayer, was their attempt to help without truly interfering. There truly is a scientific feeling to the witness of the Counsel.

I can also feel the Counsel's reactions to this man's understanding, or lack of understanding, and still the Counsel will not interfere but instead accepts the man's interpretation of their "story". The level of acceptance in the Counsel of the evolution of our planet is astounding. They truly will not interfere but will help when asked. I can strongly sense their dedication to our evolution and to their assistance where they can. Fascinating.

DR: I have to ask, who is he who wrote this down?

DS: We see a bearded man, dark-haired, humanoid, not of the consciousness of those we (the Counsel) created, but more evolved. A human being now, but of the descendants of the humanoids.

He is in the hottest part of the world, the deserts. He is a worshiper of Nature, Sun, and Moon. He is gratefully respectful of Nature, because in the arid land he lives, he must be. For Nature can destroy him.

I am having trouble seeing the timeframes. Creator of All That Is, show me again, please, the timeframes.

He is nomadic. There is a story of Messiah, but the Messiah has not arrived. At this point, the story of Messiah is a hope. Many questions are being asked about what is not working in the land, about the seeming punishments from Nature.

He is a medicine man of a tribe, seeking to see how to save the tribe from Nature's wrath. He does not write. He hears and re-tells. The story was written generations later. But it originated in his wanting to understand why the Nature, that can be so beautifully supportive, also can be so destructive.

DR: Is there a name?

DS: *I have a lot of resistance to this....* I want to use the word, Ezra. But he is also referred to in the tribe as the One. There is a sense that he is the One, because he knows the methods to hear Nature. That is all that they understand in the tribe. That is all he explains to the tribe. When he accessed our Counsel, he was one of the first to reach beyond the natures.

#7 Recording 51:39 *Ezra*

DR: In an earlier recording, a man named Ezra was mentioned, who was given an explanation for why things went badly for his tribe. He interpreted the Counsel's words as being evil. Can you explain what the Counsel said to this man, Ezra, that created this idea of evil? What was said to him?

DS: *Show me this through the Ezra's eyes please, Creator.*

Note from Donna: The words into "the" Ezra need explanation, I feel. This designation is to speak to the difference between the man of Ezra that I earlier describe in human terms. Here the use of the words "the Ezra" refers to my connecting to the higher consciousness of Ezra and the higher consciousness is not at all the same as the characteristics of the man, Ezra. It brings me to a completely different connection with Ezra, one that allows me to know him on a whole other level, beyond his humanity. The next descriptive words speak to the quality of his consciousness and less about his character. It is a different viewpoint and allows me to have a more full understanding of this man, Ezra.

When we move into the essence of the Ezra, it is strong, faithful, a bit idealized. Here, also a bit black and white. And there was a sense of peace that pervaded him in his prayer time, in his time spent in prayer to God. It calmed him and brought a peace over him. As if that is how he knew he had made connection. He was in that place of pure prayer. That is how he would see it, pure prayer.

The Counsel thought this would be a place where they could insert understandings, guidance to him. But when they did, it disturbed that prayerful peace, and he knew it was not of his prayers. And so, he took this to mean it was not of God. Not because he could sense the Counsel or knew what Counsel was, but because when these thoughts entered his head, they took away his prayerful peace. They did not come from the peace. They came, and they seemed to destroy the peace.

He lost his focus and his prayer. He lost his peace, and yet there was information left in his mind. And he had no explanation for this. And so, the explanation was made (by him).

The Counsel did not appreciate the prayerful, peaceful place he was in. They saw it as a receptive place, accessible place. They had no understanding of prayerful peace. And so did not go in carefully and there was regret. The regret is true and deep.

But a learning happened for the Counsel. They understood something else of the psychology that was developing in the humans, in the seeds of Adam. This was fascinating to them, how the consciousness had again, changed, evolved. And so even the error, *don't know if that is the right word*, even the error they made, they came away with understandings of what they were involved in and the experiment they had begun; how far it had moved and grown and evolved.

And even now as we speak to you, I can feel in the Counsel that they still do not understand prayerful peace. It is what in your language today you might call meditation. They (the Counsel) don't understand that space. They can watch humans access it, but they don't understand it. They cannot experience it, and so they do not know what it is.

And so now when they connect, as they do with this one (referring to Donna), they're very direct about it. And those they speak through know who they are and what they are doing.

They (the Counsel) in disturbing the peaceful prayer of Ezra, they learned. And it doesn't feel like they did it again. They tried different things similar to it, and then discovered that if they were to speak to these (questions), they had to speak as they were and not try to hide themselves in what was already in the beliefs (of the listener). Again, it was an attempt to stay unknown to the humans. An attempt to insert in the least … *not damaging* … intrusive way.

I can sense how the Counsel attempted to imitate Ezra's connection to his God. I can sense the Counsel's attempt to disguise themselves and use the beliefs of the listener, as they describe it. Truly the Counsel did not understand "intrusive" until they witnessed Ezra's reaction to their intrusion. I can see and sense the growth and learning this provided to the Counsel as they come to realize that they cannot disguise themselves; that if they are to communicate, they must do so as themselves.

I am left with a sense that the Counsel truly does not have the emotional disturbances that humans can experience and so cannot understand the peaceful freedom we can come to, away from our emotional disturbances. I experience them as peaceful, solid, and consistent. My experience of humans in my channeling work is of their inconsistency and their reactivity. These sensations seem to be something that the Counsel has no experience with and so it makes perfect sense to me that the Counsel still does not understand the space of prayerful peace.

The understandings that came from that time is when they (the Counsel), realized how sensitive that space the brain can get into is, and how much evolved the brain had become. And so, there were great scientific understandings and marvels from that experience, but there was also regret at what they had left with this one you have named (Ezra).

DR: What did the Counsel say to Ezra that he misinterpreted as evil existing?

DS: It wasn't what was said, but that when the thoughts were planted in his mind, the prayerful peace left. And so, he felt intruded upon, invaded.

Can we know what was said? What was it you were attempting to insert, please?

It was some kind of direction, asking for an action. It was well-intended, and the Counsel was trying to direct them away from some danger.

I can't hear the words or see the specifics. But they were trying to make them safer, steer them away from some danger. But what matters in all of this is not what was said but was the awareness in Ezra that the prayerful peace was destroyed, and thoughts were placed in his mind. He felt invaded, intruded, frightened, and then the Counsel realized the sensitivity of how the brain was developing. And so, I cannot see the words or the message. But the feeling I have when I ask of it, is that it was something to direct them to a place of greater safety, as if there was a danger coming.

DR: It seemed like he felt he was being misdirected by some entity that wasn't positive.

DS: Yes, because every time he had ever been guided by the God, the prayerful peace deepened and strengthened, and he was left with a sense of caring support. When this occurred, all that disappeared, and he felt as if that which was inserted into his mind had destroyed it (the prayerful peace). And then he felt vulnerable and frightened, very frightened.

DR: This was the beginning of the idea of evil or an evil force on the planet?

DS: It was at a time where this thread we are seeing in several of the stories we have spoken of, was now present, and the sensitivity of the humans through their belief systems and trust of what they called God was really developing. And so when things happened that were unexplainable, as with Ezra, there then began the labeling of it as something else.

That something else was seen as very powerful and so frightening, because Ezra was unable to stop the thoughts from being placed in his mind. And that is from where the fear came. That is where the "demon" was born, because when such evil, as it came to be called, occurred, there was no tracking how it could have happened or from where it could have come. And so, if there was not prayerful peace around guidance, there was great fear and skepticism. It needed to be in the prayerful place, in the protection of God. **It was the seeds of**

some changes in the evolution of the humans.

DR: Last question, this was the "seeds" of evil, of the devil, of the fallen angel?

DS: **Fallen angel, not yet. Devil, not yet. But the beginning of...we can use the word demon.** For some reason we can't yet come to what was later defined as the devil, because it feels as if the demon is a worker of the devil. And so, they are first aware of what they are calling the demons before they become aware of the devil.

And not until they were aware of the devil could they become aware of how could the devil be, and so the fallen angel story arises. It is as if the demon is the worker or the soldier of the devil, and so they only first meet the workers of the devil which they call demons, before they come to the devil itself.

*As I am viewing the development of these beliefs that lead to the definitions of evil, demon, devil and fallen angel, I can see a timeline in this development. It is as if I am viewing the historic timeline of these new definitions and can feel how they are clearly defined, and how one then leads to the next. Each time, there is a search to explain a cause for the changes being experienced; and, each time, that leads to new labels, new definitions, and new connections. First evil, then demon, that then leads to devil that then leads to fallen angel. Each is a story. Each is an attempt to explain changes that are not understood. **Each is an attempt to place blame outside for what is developing inside.** How the mind labels and creates to explain is so very clear to me in this timeline. Fascinating how powerful our creative mind is and fascinating how we can convince ourselves that what the mind creates then becomes the "truth". Amazing!*

One more moment, there is this sense of connection…

Part of the demon-devil was connected to that black thread that was being born in the psychology of the humans; that selfish, prideful, competitive, destructive, sometimes violent, careless thread. That thread that had inserted itself into the psychology now. Part of the demon-devil-fallen angel story was an attempt to explain something that was unexplainable at that stage of man. As if there needed to be an outside cause for what was clearly an inside growth, an inside evolution in the psychology.

That black thread strengthened separation, because selfishness became more important, and self-serving became more important, and careless. To be self-serving, you needed to be careless, without compassion. And these behaviours were so abhorrent. How could this be present within our tribe, within us? How could these thoughts be present?

And so, when, in attempt to look for an outside source, not considering an inside source, that again is where the demon-devil-fallen angel story is fleshed out more. Because there was, from the Counsel's perspective as I'm seeing it, this growth when they left Eden; this growth of self, self-care, looking after self, needing food, needing shelter. Looking after your own family, not necessarily the tribe. There were these things that started to separate what was originally the one tribe, and it was the needs of the self.

As that separation strengthened, this thread, we'll call it a black thread, of self and separation was getting stronger. And so, the whole demon-devil story was an attempt to understand what was in actuality, an evolution in the mind, of a separate ego, of separation, of no longer being part of one mind or one tribe, but the separate self. And, as that id or that ego started to evolve in the psychology of the humans, those who still remembered the way of the beginning, were desperate to understand how this could occur. How they could be more separate? <u>How could some of them be so separate from God, when they all came from the original place?</u>

And so that is what fueled, *that is the best word*, that is what fueled that whole demon beginning. And then, as that black thread of separate self, selfishness continued to grow, it gave birth to demon to devil, and from devil to fallen angel. It actually feels like demon-devil came before the fallen angel story.

DR: Then, simply mankind created the whole mythology of a fallen angel?

DS: Yes, to explain something that was completely unexplainable to them. To explain behaviour that was out of character, that wasn't in generations before, but was in the younger generations. It was there, and it hadn't been in the older generations. How could this happen? There must be a blame. There must be a cause. And there wasn't the strength of mind to consider an internal cause, so they sought an external cause. And so, the stories of demon-devil-and fallen angel were created, because they could not fathom that there was an internal cause. *This now feels complete.*

Discussion

THE MYTH OF EVIL

#2 Recording 1:13:27 *Counsel's Mistake*

DS: It was really interesting. I am perfectly willing to be wrong, but when you asked specifically who this man was that wanted to understand the changes in the natural world, I could see him.

He was a little man. I am going to say he was four feet tall, medium build, dark, dark eyes, hair, and beard. He wasn't monkeyish at all. He was draped in layers because of the heat. And he felt like the medicine man, or the religious man, and he truly had his sincere heart wanting to understand why nature was being so destructive, and was there any way to protect his tribe? I want to say the Counsel spoke to him, because he was so <u>sincerely</u> trying to understand the nature of life. But he took everything they told him to be the specific answer to his question. And that is where the error took place. And so that is where the labels (of evil) got put on the story. The Counsel would never use those words.

DR: It was amazing that a person then, with no training or background, would be able to have enough consciousness to reach out or to receive from the Counsel.

DS: It felt like the Counsel responded to the purity of his desire to help his tribe. It wasn't a selfish request. It was pure in its intent. And it's the purity they responded to. And possibly, they made a mistake in what they thought he would understand. I don't know. But it was his purity that caused them to reach out to him. And my sense is that it was more like they gave to him. He had a vision quest or had a vision as opposed to a conversation.

#2 Recording 1:21:54 *The One*

DS: But the first name was *the One*. I would say that's what everyone called him, *the One*. Maybe because he was the one who could access, I don't know. But then when I actually looked for a name, Ezra was the name I heard. But everyone who spoke of him, spoke of him as "the One" in the tribe itself. It felt like a desert tribe. But I couldn't tell you what continent.

#7 Recording 1:11:03 *Beginnings of Evil*

DS: It was fascinating to me because it feels like <u>it's the</u>

beginning of what is defined in our religions as evil. But what it felt like to me was the beginning of the id, of the ego, of those layers of the psychology; as if that was starting to develop. There were selfish thoughts; there were separate from God thoughts; there was questioning of what had always been done. And that led to misbehaviour. There wasn't the consciousness to consider that it was an internal development, and so there had to be someone or something to blame. And that's where I could clearly see that the demon was the first level, and then demons, because they seemed to multiply. They then were working for a devil. And then the devil had to have come from somewhere, and then came the fallen angel story.

But it feels like it was all originating in the unexplainable violent selfish behaviours, in hatreds that were coming in, and deeper and deeper separations that were coming in, deeper and deeper violent competitions that were developing.

It feels to me, although I don't know enough about it, like it was something developing in the psychology of us, like the id or the ego. As that developed, there was this sense of 'no, me first'. That idea hadn't been in the original beginnings, because the consciousness brought by the Counsel didn't have this. This is again where what the Counsel introduced into the Earth started to evolve in its own manner. And because the Counsel was hands off, they let it evolve. This was a step in our evolution. But it was so unexplainable at the time, that the leaders of the tribe had to come up with something. "How could God let this happen?" "God didn't let this happen. The devil did it." I am oversimplifying, it but that's what it feels like to me.

Section Three

NOAH -
NO ANGRY GOD

The Biblical story of Noah begins as follows:

This is the line of Noah. Noah was a righteous man; he was blameless in his age; Noah walked with God. (Genesis 6: 9)

When God saw how corrupt the earth was, for all flesh had corrupted its ways on earth, God said to Noah, "I have decided to put an end to all flesh, because the earth is filled with lawlessness because of them: I am about to destroy them with the earth. Make yourself an ark of gopher wood..." (Genesis 6:12-14)

For my part, I am about to bring the flood – waters upon the earth - to destroy all flesh under the sky in which there is breath of life; everything on earth shall perish. (Genesis 6:17)

And of all that lives, of all flesh, you shall take two of each into the ark to keep alive with you; they shall be male and female. From birds of every kind, cattle of every kind, every kind of creeping thing on earth, two of each shall come with you to stay alive. (Genesis 6:19:21)

Noah did so, just as God commanded him, so he did. (Genesis 6:22)

DR: A second Noah story in the Bible is slightly different. In that version, *Noah is commanded to take seven pairs of clean animals, not just two pairs, into the ark, along with one pair of unclean animals.* (Genesis 7:1-5)

Again, like the creation story of Adam and Eve, two different versions of the Noah story exist.

Aside from the slightly different versions, the modern reader would find many issues with this story. One example is that many would discount it in its entirety. Others might go to great lengths and verbal gymnastics to try to explain it rationally.

It is impossible to explain how Noah and his family could gather pairs of all the millions of species from all over the Earth and keep them separated and alive for forty days at sea. And there is no mention of food-bearing plants being saved on the ship so that crops could be planted after the waters subsided. It may also be impossible for the waters of the earth to completely cover the earth unless most of the mountains were flattened. In that case, to where would the waters recede?

Because the story as written is so difficult to accept, I asked questions to see if there was a man named Noah who built a great ship. If there was flooding on a large scale, were animals rescued from drowning? The answers from the channel did not surprise me, even if I could not have predicted them in advance.

#4 Recording 26:36 *Story of the Flood*

DR: Can you explain the whole story of Noah and the flood?

DS: It **does not** feel, as my senses are allowed to participate, that there was one Noah and one ark. There was a climate shift out of a cold spell, and there was much melting. There were tsunamis and the animals gathered in the high points, because their instincts were keen, and the men paid attention. There were rafts and ships built, and animals, as well as humans, were put aboard in various places.

The sensation is that there is water running down the globe in all directions. **It was not punishment from a Lord or God.** It was climate. But again, the minds without knowledge and without control, attributed it to behaviour and as a punishment. And the story was created.

The truth of the story is that animals were saved, not whole herds, but pairs, because there were small ships and small rafts. And so you could not save a herd; you had to save pairs in the herd that would help the herd survive. It was not a coordinated effort; it was reactive to the climate around the globe. And that is why there are stories in your myths and tales of various floods, because it was a climate event.

Interesting, when I feel the movement of the water, it seems to stop at the equator. As if there were not similar floods in the southern part of the globe, but only in the northern hemisphere of the globe. It feels as if it was climate and tied to the plate movements in some way.

DR: Does that mean that the humans and animals had some sort of communication for humans to rescue some of the animals?

DS: No, it was of necessity. If the waters were getting deeper and the animals were allowed on the raft, then the animals went on the raft. But the humans were careful not to allow a whole herd. There was more of a rescue happening. Animals being retrieved from small rocks and water. It doesn't feel communicated or organized. It feels reactive, rescuing.

DR: But this was widespread?

DS: In the northern hemisphere it happened. The image is a waterfall coming down from the north. It was not continuous or one waterfall, but waters falling and tsunamis and climate meltings, great meltings. Then there were reactions to the meltings. There was weather. We will not say there was no storm, but the rain was not the only cause.

DR Was there at that time massive melting of glaciers or the poles?

DS: Yes. There was just this climate event. Ice melted and rain fell, and ice melted, and plates moved and earthquakes and tsunamis and ... It doesn't feel like there was an exterior cause. I can't see a meteor hitting or anything like that. It was a climate event.

I can also softly sense the confusion and fear in the humans. I can feel their reaction to the fact that it is happening to them and is completely beyond their control.

DR: Were a lot of the animals and many of the humans, and humanoids destroyed?

DS: Yes, there was definitely a culling of the beings on your planet. We would say near thirty or forty percent.

Different areas saved different animals, because they were the animals that mattered to them. They were the animals of the region, and they were the animals that needed the rescuing. They were the animals found. So, it did create extinctions, but not mass extinctions. Perhaps thirty percent, some areas forty percent.

It simplified your world. That was the result as we witnessed it. When the waters receded, and the climate settled, and everyone settled, the world was simpler, and there were fewer in the animal world. There was also a different relationship between the humans and nature.

The uncontrollableness of the event is where the stories came from. By this stage in the evolution of mankind, accepting what was out of their control was frightening. And so, stories were made. Gods, nature stories were invented to explain what was out of their control. And that is where the myths and mythologies, the stories began.

DR: Did this happen in one time period, or did it happen repeatedly over centuries?

DS: It feels like it was an event. *Show me the timelines, please.* It feels like it happened in various places, not all at the same time, but the same cause. And it took perhaps a year to complete. There was this continuous movement and melting. And it would be stronger on this side and then stronger on that side of the Earth. It was pretty continuous, but never continuous in the one same place.

It was about a year, four or five seasons as you would call it now. But the feeling I have when I use the word "seasons" is as if it was a long winter and then there was a long summer. They weren't the seasons as you call them now. And so, there was a year of a long winter and then a very long summer. That's when the melting started, and then the summer lasted longer.

There was a lot of freezing in the long winter, and then there were two long summers. If we had to put a time frame to it, it might have been eighteen months or twenty-two months by your calendar now. But it was more about the climate change. There was the cold and then there was warm, and then there was hot and that was when the melting occurred. And so, it wasn't continuous in any one place, but it was continuous around the northern hemisphere. If we put your time frame to it, we would say a year and a half, not quite two years.

DR: Then did people, and animals too, have to survive on boats or rafts for days or weeks or months?

DS: Yes, and then it would recede, and they would settle, and then it would come back. They kept the boats for a long time, because they didn't understand how it happened. They didn't understand how it would end. But they weren't on the rafts and boats too long. It feels more like weeks than months. There was a lot of death, animals and humans, humanoids.

DR: Food must have been very scarce.

DS: Yes, but because it happened in sections at a time, when food here was gone, then food was still there. It changed where the tribes went. It changed how the tribes fed themselves. It changed the size of the herds of the animals. The behaviour afterwards was very adaptive.

There was no orchestration from us in this; it was a planetary evolution. One of the things we find most fascinating about the Earth is her ability to evolve. There's an aliveness in her evolution. And this climate event was part of her evolution as a planetary space.

#4 Recording 39:14 *Earth's Unique Evolution*

DR: It seems as if the Earth is unique in its evolution?

DS: Definitely yes, that's the feeling we have. As I connect to the Counsel, when they witnessed evolution on the planet, that's what made the planet so special, so intriguing, so interesting. It's what drew different councils to the planet, this unique evolutionary ability. I cannot say it doesn't exist any place else, but those that have interacted with the planet have not seen it elsewhere.

#8 Recording 24:43 *Story of the Flood*

DR: We talked before about the Flood, the Great Flood. Was

there actually a man named Noah?

DS: We are not sensing a man of that name. We are sensing two or three men of that purpose, trying to save parts of seeds and animals, plants, from the floods as they increased. We are not sensing one ark. Though we are sensing three different ships, large enough to be called ships. We are sensing several who had visions at different times of the waters and followed those visions.

We would say in your story of Noah, there are three or four timelines, in three or four different places on the planet where very similar behaviour occurred. And these visionaries and shipbuilders became the story of Noah.

DR: Were these three, any one of them or all three, from the lineage of Adam and Eve?

DS: All were from the lineage of Adam and Eve.

The first story, similar to the Noah story, did not come from the tribes of Adam and Eve. It came from someone else. A humanoid. A blond storyteller, a music player, the court's entertainer. He traveled and met two or three of these visionaries. He was allowed onto one of the ships. And it feels like he was the first one to formulate the story. And then from that, someone else took that and created the story you know as Noah and the Ark. It is based in truth, but it is an exaggerated truth in the Noah story.

DR: This man who recorded this envisioned the ships? He visited the ship after the flood?

DS: He was traveling. It feels like the floods did not occur all at the same place, at the same time. He was traveling ahead of the waters and happened to meet two men in a row, who had a similar vision. Because after meeting the first one, and he had seen the waters and escaped with his life, he took the second one seriously, and asked to be taken on the ship. And that was the beginning of him creating a song-story about it.

He feels blond. It feels as if he carries an instrument, as if he is a storyteller. In another part of the world, he might be called a gypsy. He was a court entertainer, but he had fallen from favour and that is why he was traveling when the floods started.

The floods were consecutive, but not all at the same time and so there was perhaps months between them. There were three definitely, maybe four, different areas of flooding. Feels like there was definitely two ships, maybe three. I'm not seeing a fourth.

DR: The man who recorded this was actually on one of the ships during a flood?

DS: He chose to ask to be allowed to be on the ship, because he had heard of a vision of the previous shipmaker, and had laughed at it as others had. And then, he barely escaped with his life.

So when he heard this vision again, he took it seriously, and asked to be allowed on the ship. Of course, he was. It was the humane thing to do. And while on the ship he started to create his song-story, because it helped those on the ship believe. <u>It helped them feel protected by their god, to know that another</u>

had seen the same vision, and that there had been those saved there as well.

It (the story) sort of started out as an entertainment, but then the reality of it having happened twice, confirmed by this young man, seeded in their beliefs a sense of supportedness by God force. It strengthened their belief in the visionary. That's how it worked its way into the stories of your Bible, because it did serve to strengthen their faith. It just did not happen exactly as it was told. But it served the faith of these men and women very strongly. It strengthened the original beliefs of the tribes. It helped them believe again, shall we say, in the old ways.

I can feel the strength of the desire of the Counsel for us to understand how positively influencing that storyteller was. He helped those of faith to feel rescued instead of punished.

So, this young man, inadvertently, sharing what he thought was in fun and entertainment, created a story that became a very serious part of their beliefs.

What is most interesting here is how his "song-story" began as entertainment on the ship. I can feel how deeply his story is affecting the people. I can feel that it strengthens their faith in the visionary. I can then feel how it goes even farther to strengthen the beliefs that are connected to the "old ways". As I witness this emotional reaction within the people on this ship, I can completely understand why the "story of Noah" for the Bible would have been created. If this simple story nurtured such faith, then a grander story could have a grander effect. It feels like a decision was made for the people of faith. The biblical "story of Noah" truly has a truth within it, but it has been made grander for reasons of faith and encouragement.

DR: So how many people were aboard this ship that he was on?

DS: We would say a village of four, five families. *Show me numbers, please.*

When I see the ship, it feels like it's the village, but they are not all related. Perhaps four families that have commonality, relatedness, and then perhaps two other families that were in service to the village, but not connected in a familial way. We would say perhaps forty. When we see the heads, we would say forty.

DR: This ship, did it have oars or sails? How was it moved?

DS: It had oars. It had roofed-in areas. It was sturdy. What I am seeing, it has oars. But it feels like everyone that is on it is protected, even the oarsmen, as if there are wooden roofs, or roofs of some type. It's quite wide and almost flat-bottomed, so it's very sturdy. It's long, but it is very wide. It feels like it was wooden.

DR: The construction, especially the bottom, was this logs or planks, boards?

DS: We perceive it as planks. It feels like planks, but some of them are quite rough. They did not have the time to do what they would do if they had a year to make a boat. It feels like they were more finished on the inside than on the outside. They feel more like planks or halved trunks of trees, with some finishings to make it waterproof. It does feel like it was rushed. It doesn't feel like they had forty days and forty nights.

DR: How long in advance of the flood did they have to make this?

DS: Three weeks, 21 days, 30 days, *I'm not sure*, but the one who held the vision acted quickly. We would say within 48 hours this one started to make plans. And there were some other signs in nature. There were short spells of heavy storms that helped to convince others of the possibility of the truth. There were storms for two or three days, and then it stopped for a week and then storms again, heavy storms, with waters raising, plates shifting, earthquakes, water.

We can see a storm comes for three days that helps convince others to help him, to pitch in. And then the storm clears for a week and then the storm comes back with an earthquake.

I can feel the hurry. I can see and feel how the inconsistent weather events hurried the construction along and convinced others to help. I am witnessing and can feel from the Earth herself, how the volatility is increasing, and it has a strong effect on the people in their preparations.

It was just the volatileness on the Earth herself, in the weathers and on the land that helped everyone to hurry for this. Whether they were protecting themselves from water or the land or the weather. It didn't matter at some point. That is why it might have been flat-bottomed, so that they would have a sturdy place in water or on land. It feels flat-bottomed to me.

The floods were effective in how they brought the people together and how they strengthened their faith in the old ways. It is amazing how this almost feels orchestrated. As if this whole "story" in its creation and inclusion in the Bible, feels like CREATION itself was involved in some way. I cannot explain that further. It is simply a feeling, an observation that this whole thing has such a sense of a "higher" orchestration to events. Something beyond the Earth, Mankind and Nature. What that is, I cannot say.

#8 Recording 36:09 *God of Wrath*

DR: Can you explain the image of the angry God who caused the flood and who destroyed Sodom and Gomorrah, this wrathful angry god image?

DS: There was fear of nature, the unreliability of the Earth, the earthquakes, and the unpredictable weather, out of its normal pattern. There was fear of the end of the world. There was not an understanding of what or why this occurred. And those who gave into their fears, created these type of stories, punishment stories, looking for blame, looking for a source of why.

This is why the story is important. The faith was jeopardized through this time. Such upheaval, uncontrollable natural upheaval had not been experienced by these tribes. And they had no understanding of it, and so they created understandings, stories, punishments, blamings.

This is why, when the man came from the other ship, he helped to restore their faith that they hadn't been abandoned; they weren't being punished. That, in fact, the vision had saved them. It helped to quiet some of the stories of punishment, but not all of the stories, for free will was quite strong by this point. And those who were most afraid, those who had the most number of secret sins, they are the ones who created the stories.

Fascinating to hear that those of "secret sins" were the ones who created stories of punishment. I call it fascinating, because I can feel the scientific fascination of the Counsel as they witness, realize, and understand this next step in the development of our will and mind.

DS: *Looking to see if we can see the source of Sodom and Gomorrah.*

We are taken to stones. We are taken to someone who has had a nightmare, and imagines something in the stone.

The one who initiated the Sodom and Gomorrah story really, truly thought they saw a being in the stone. They were waking from a nightmare, and the nightmare carried into their vision awake. And they ran to warn the others that now something was happening in the stone. But it was of their own shall we call it, "sinful nature", their own nightmares, their own secrets.

This was a life-changing time for many. It highlighted those of weaker faith. It strengthened those of stronger faith. It healed those of weaker faith. It was a time where faith of the original tribe somehow came reborn. As if the stories had never been in the history before, so why were they here now? What was the weakness now? What was the cause now? It did lend a strictness to the believers, and a healing of the penance to those who had been losing faith.

DR: Were these two towns or cities actually destroyed by natural events?

DS: Yes, completely.

The Counsel has a viewpoint of this. *One moment, please. How I have been speaking thus far, I have been seeing the events, but now I can feel Counsel has a viewpoint.* The Counsel viewed this time.

We witnessed the changes in the Earth and knew that the planet itself was shifting and changing. We would not interfere, but did try to facilitate where we could, but had very little effect.

We were fascinated by the development, the dynamic within what you are calling the tribes. Their relationship to nature changed. Their relationship to a god they came to believe in changed. The relationships in the families changed.

It was the first demonstration where we could actually see into the secrets. This event, that gave birth to the story of Noah and the Ark, its true importance was that there had been secrets in people. And this revealed the secrets. It frightened them enough to reveal their secrets, their sins, their selfishnesses, their lies. And we found it fascinating to witness.

First, we watched the birth of secrecy and lies, of deceit. And then this event seemed to frighten them in such a way that all the deceit and secrets came to the surface. As if in penance, in fear, they revealed all.

And then the aftermath was a tightening of the regulations, a tightening of the tribe. Not in an iron fist kind of way, but more supportive. As if they saw weakness where those were deceitful and where those were selfish. Perhaps there wasn't enough support in the tribe. So, it changed the dynamic of the tribe. It changed the dynamic of the relationship to the god. It changed the dynamic of the families. We will not say that there was no secrecy or deceit afterwards. But much of the secrecy and deceit was revealed, and there was a time of honesty. There was a strengthening of the old ways that were originally in the Eden space, and it did lend an honesty to the tribes. <u>It was the birth of a deeper level of honesty in the tribes.</u>

This was a very frightening event to the people who lived through it. And it was changing the dynamic of the human relationship. That change happened very quickly; it was astounding how quickly the evolutionary adaptation within the tribes and family to such an event occurred. The evaluation, the intelligence, and then the evolution, and the compensation. The internal dynamics, relationship dynamics, shifted greatly in this time.

Camaraderie deepened, honesty deepened, mutual support deepened, and the rules strengthened. It was the creation of penance. There was the creation of mercy. There were new ideas expressed, and it seemed to come out of this fearful time, when the threat was so uncontrollable, so impossible to escape.

#8 Recording 45:40 *God of Wrath, The Results*

DR: These events (the floods, the destruction of Sodom and Gomorrah) gave them an idea of a watchful, wrathful god which actually helped them to be more honest, and more faithful?

DS: It feels as if it … *as I am perceiving it through the Counsel's viewpoint…* it feels as if the families became stronger, as if those who were deceitful, those who were secret-ing, weren't getting enough support. It feels like it did strengthen and make more strict laws. <u>But it also seemed to strengthen the dynamic of the tribe, the mutual support within the tribe, within the</u>

families.

It is fascinating to watch fear create the openings that it did. This opening, started in fear and then grew, dare I say evolved, into something very different. It truly changes the dynamics of the tribe, that had a ripple effect for many generations.

DR: By turning these natural cataclysmic events into ones that were caused by God, this was actually quite helpful at that time.

DS: Exactly, and it feels as if this was witnessed by Counsel, but not interfered with. *And when I go higher to CREATION:*

CREATION is also watching the evolution of creation, of the creation Earth, of the creation human, of the creation man. CREATION, itself, is just allowing this to take place. There isn't the feeling of a hand involved. It is the Earth, in her own natural evolution, affecting the evolution and dynamics of the tribes.

The feeling is of CREATION itself understanding the very nature of EVOLUTION on the Earth and the changes that come from it. But these understandings are not of a scientific mind. These understandings have an appreciation in them, a joy in them, and an acceptance of how creations create. I can say that CREATION, has a feel that is so different from anything else I have experienced before.

CREATION is interested in us. CREATION is loving that we as creations are creating, are evolving. The joy, the amazement is tangible. And it leaves me feeling truly supported and loved in a way that is so not human.

Discussion

NOAH

#8 Recording 1:10:11 *Flood Changed Dynamics of Belief*

DS: The beginnings of deceit were fascinating to watch. In the questions around Noah, I was aware that some of these people around Noah had secrets and deceit. And I could actually feel the presence of them. It felt like it was one in twenty. It wasn't nineteen out of twenty. But with this cataclysmic event, it made them afraid of their secrets; made them afraid they were to blame. They were afraid that they had sinned, and so they became afraid that their lives had been part of the cause of this cataclysmic event.

Again, it changed the dynamics of belief and actually reinforced belief. But it seemed to come about in a very innocent and natural way. When I checked with the Counsel and then I checked with CREATION to see if they had a hand in it? There was no hand in it. It was just EVOLUTION. It was simply evolution, and it was the evolution of the dynamic of human. It is fascinating for me, for I can see how we came to be as we are today. Fascinating...so interesting.

Section Four

ABRAHAM &
SARAH - NO
SACRIFICE OF SON

The Biblical story of Abraham and Sarah starts with the journey towards Canaan.

Terah took his son Abram, his grandson Lot, the son of Haran, and his daughter-in-law Sarai, the wife of his son Abram, and they set out together from Ur of the Chaldeans for the land of Canaan; but when they had come as far as Haran, they settled there. (Genesis 11:31)

After Terah died, Abram's journey continued. The LORD said to Abram, "Go forth from your native land and from your father's house to the land that I will show you." (Genesis 12:1) Abram went forth as the Lord had commanded him, and Lot went with him. (Genesis 12:4)

DR: This story seemingly has many unclear facets, being inconsistent and discontinuous. First of all, there is no reason given for Terah and Abraham to leave Ur and head to Canaan. Why Canaan? Secondly, why do they settle in Haran if Terah, the head of the tribe, wanted to go to Canaan? Thirdly, why do they continue on the journey just after Terah dies, and does God speak up then and tell Abraham to "go to a land" but doesn't specify which one?

In the story of Abraham, I wanted to know why he left Ur for Canaan, what his relationship was to Melchizedek, and clarifications of their time in Egypt. Of the latter, I was interested in Abraham's role in Egypt, the sister/wife confusion over Sarah, and why they eventually left Egypt. The issue of the relationship between Abraham and Melchizedek (Genesis 14:18-20) was most intriguing to me and was a prime reason why I started this endeavour in the first place. Extremely puzzling to me was why Abraham, after a successful military rescue and campaign, gave homage to a mysterious person who appeared only once in the Bible.

Chapter Seven

IN UR

Abram and Nahor took to themselves wives, the name of Abram's wife being Sarai and that of Nahor's wife Milcah, the daughter of Haran, the father of Milcah and Iscah. Now Sarai was barren, she had no child. (Genesis 11:29-30)

The Hebrew Bible only has one brief mention of the marriage of Abraham and Sarah (initially named Abram and Sarai). The following section tells a much more involved and detailed story of Abraham and Sarah prior to and including their marriage (excerpts from Women in the Hebrew Bible: Their Stories)

#4 Recording 18:25 *Abraham's Family Residing in Ur*

DR: Was Abraham and family living in the city of Ur?

DS: They were first in a quiet place, not hiding exactly, but in a quiet village near Ur. They would visit Ur, or they would go to the markets of Ur, but they didn't live there. There was this simplicity in the living. Abraham's father wanted some solitude. It would be equated to someone living in the country instead of the city, though that is an oversimplification. Ur was not what you would call the city in your day and time now, but it was still busier, more people. As Abraham reached youthful manhood, there was a sense of movement to Ur for education, temple, there were reasons pertinent to Abraham's upbringing. It doesn't feel like his family lived there; he moved there. Then there were connections to the tribes; there were connections to the teachers, religious connections, spiritual connections, and it did become his home. When he created his family with the marriage of Sarah, he stayed there. It feels as if he moved his mother there after his father's death, out of duty, out of love. We can say yes to your question.

#4 Recording 20:52 *Sarah and Her Family Residing in Ur*

DR: So, Sarah and her family were from the same area in Ur or nearby?

DS: Abraham's father's home was west of Ur and Sara's family's home was east. Unlike Abraham's father, they were not in the country and solitude. They were perhaps in a small village, not as big as Ur is, but it still would be called the village. It wasn't isolated. They did come to Ur for certain celebrations.

#4 Recording 21:56 *Abraham's Education in Ur*

DR: So, there was a temple in Ur that Abraham went to? What kind of religious practices were there?

DS: It was for education, that the elders held meetings not classes. Meetings for the young men to help them find their way, find their place in the tribe. There were prayer times, where they would pray together, the prayer space of vision. Those young men that were adept at the vision space of prayer were taught more often and Abraham was one of these. These were not the elders that would have allowed the women to be taught or even recognized as having visions in prayer space. This was done quietly among the women themselves.

Abraham was chosen and educated but it was like meetings rather than classes. There was strictness, expectations, and many rules. Abraham did struggle with the rules. But he did see improvement in his visions and a stronger sense of God in his heart and so he obeyed, because he found results. Once he became his own man, he did change the rules, for some of them did not make sense to him, and did not seem to improve situations.

DR: So, this school was taught by people like the Hebrews? They didn't worship the local gods?

DS: No, this was the Hebrew elders and the elder they were, the more status they had in the teaching. They were maintaining the beliefs, maintaining the history, maintaining the stories. Abraham was not a storyteller, because his visions took him another direction, but these men also trained the storytellers.

#4 Recording 27:10 *Beliefs of the Elders*

DR: So, these tribes were teaching about the same beliefs that Abraham had. They were teaching him about one God and the whole belief system?

DS: They were perpetuating the Eden beliefs. They were perpetuating the simplicity, the honour, the integrity, but it was also starting to expand as we have spoken of before. EVOLUTION had influenced the growth and it influenced the faith and had influenced what prayer space was becoming. So, our interest (the interest of the Counsel) was there because of the influence of the evolution. There is a sense, and we (the Counsel) traced it, of a continuous growth in beliefs and we began to see evolution's influence on the beliefs, and we watched it grow. It was about how to live; how to serve God; and this was the beginning of what God wanted in service. This was near the beginning of the rules. The rules first showed themselves in the meetings with the elders. **There was a desperateness in the elders to maintain the history through the family lines and the rules came from that.** We are saying the dance, the weaving between evolution and the beliefs and holding the history, we (The Counsel) could monitor it. It was as if we could see the weavings of strings, weaving into new directions.

#2 Recording 25:37 *Raising and Training of Sarah*

DR: We wanted to talk about the Matriarchs in the Bible starting with Sarah.

You gave us previous information about her, can you expand upon that, her personality? First of all, how did she come to meet and marry Abraham?

DS: This one was very bright as a child, a little outspoken, clever; she questioned, wanted to learn. She found her way into the meetings of her father and the elders and questioned them of their studies. When she was young, she did this. She was young enough to be taken lightly and not offensively by the males. And so, her spark was recognized at a young age.

One in the circle of her father deemed her very worthy of his son. We want to say that her marriage was arranged when she was under the age of 5, 6 years old (*said surprisingly*) because the friend of her father recognized the spark within her and thought she would challenge his son and support his son well.

Her craving to have knowledge of the ways to live, it mattered to this one. It was never considered that she would be taught as the boys were taught, but it was admired that she wanted to learn. And so, she was betrothed to Abraham early. This was not Abraham's father; this was one of the circle of her father. But it was not the father of Abraham, it was the one who knew of Abraham and knew the mother of Abraham. And so, the idea of the betrothal was actually brought to Abraham's mother.

Again, Abraham was young, and it was at first rejected by her. Abraham was not faithful enough for such a wife in his young years. And it feels to us as if that betrothal for Sarah was held, in that Sarah was held for Abraham. But we want to say she was much older in her marriage to Abraham than was the norm. As if Abraham's mother was waiting for something in her son to appear, to let her know that he could be married to such a woman.

She befriended Sarah, trained Sarah as a woman. Without interfering with Sarah's mother, she added to Sarah's teachings those things that the men would not teach her. Sarah was educated for nearly ten years. Sarah was educated by the mother of Abraham, her own mother, and other very wise women. We want to say other very wise women was of the red tent. *(This is a symbolic reference to the gathering of women to live separate, apart from the men, during their menstruation times.)*

She was taught many things that most women would not have been. And there was a sense of her being prepared. Though the mother of Abraham would not know, or name, speak, what Sarah was being prepared for, there was a sense of preparation ongoing. It was accepted by all those concerned, and even with Sarah herself. For Sarah had already begun the visions. Her faith was deep and in her prayer space she had already begun to have visions. She did not share them at first with anyone. And then, as the teachings with Abraham's mother engaged, she shyly shared one. And from that, more teachings arrived.

Her visions were encouraged. Her prayer space encouraged. Though neither her mother nor the mother of Abraham understood the power in Sarah's prayer space, it was encouraged. They often prayed with her to keep her safe and ensure that the visions were of God, were of that which is right. By the time Abraham was ready for Sarah, she was well-developed. She was older than most wives would have been at marriage, near thirty when she was married. It does not feel like it was a young marriage, and she was well-educated. She could question Abraham and hold her ground with Abraham and help him to establish what he came to be. She held a faith with him and a faith in him, but she also challenged him; at times she found him wanting in his faith and would challenge him so. There were times it was deemed disrespectful by the men of Abraham and his circle. But Abraham understood her love as well as her faith. And a love did grow.

They did not fall in love when they were married, but a love did grow, and it grew from their faith. It also grew from shared memories for as Abraham accessed the memories, the prayer space of Sarah also deepened, and she had glimpses of memories as well. She was never really able to put full body to them, but she knew what they were and where they came from, and for her whole life she worked on strengthening and allowing more of those memories to come through. She knew of Eden, she saw it, she felt it in her memories. In her prayer space she worked to develop it quietly. It would not have been accepted by Abraham nor his circle that she did such a thing. But it proved very useful to Abraham as the decades moved by, because they became confirmation to one another. She could sometimes confirm what he had seen, feel the strength of his faith in what he had seen and encourage him in it.

There was power in her. There was voice in her. But there was great respect and a humble faithfulness. We would not call this one a sacrificial female, but she had power. It was, from the Counsel's perspective, intriguing to see her grow this way and to see her complement Abraham. We (the Counsel) had no interference with that and cannot state to where that graceful complement came from. But as we witnessed it grow, it seemed orchestrated to us, and we have yet to discover if it was orchestrated and by what or whom. We have no science to that.

These last statements are channeled from the Counsel directly, and from that we realize that much of the information about Sarah that has been relayed here has come through Donna from the Counsel's witness of Sarah and her growth. Interesting that the Counsel is "intrigued" by the sense of orchestration that surrounds Sarah, and yet they have no "science to that". Interesting to witness the Counsel and its limitations.

#2 Recording 34:46 *Sarah's Role in the Tribe*

DR: What was Sarah's role with the beginnings of the Hebrews?

DS: Her first influence was with the females. The second influence was with some of the males that were close to Abraham because they recognized her importance to him and how she nurtured his confidence and shared his faith. He, Abraham, offered her deep respect and so those close to him were obliged to do the same, when some of them would not naturally do so. But there was something in her that commanded that respect.

Her influence was with the females. She encouraged them to be stronger, to address themselves with more decisiveness, to be a little bit more in leadership, not leaders for that was not what the women were to be, but to be supportive of the leadership within their husbands, less subservient. She did not nurture sacrifice in the females that were within her influence and so she created a strength in the females of the tribe at that time. She demonstrated to them her support of Abraham in his weaker days, shared with them her belief in Abraham and shared with them demonstrations to show how her faith in Abraham, strengthened Abraham. She taught this to them so that it was something that was taught from the mothers to the daughters, to the granddaughters; that the women had an importance to be strong with the males of that time. They had an importance in the tribe; their strength strengthened the tribe. They were not subservient. They were not servants. They were active participants and acted in the faith, for she encouraged them in the prayer space.

There were not many who wanted to learn vision, to allow vision, but those that wanted to learn she would show. There was never one that had visions the way Sarah did, but they wanted to learn. Those that wanted to learn were taught. Not many wanted to learn, for there was fear of the visions in the females. They wanted to leave the visions to Abraham and to the men of the circle. But Sarah's influence was in strengthening the female role, strengthening the wife role in the marriage, strengthening the mother role in the family, strengthening and creating a role in the tribe itself. And then the influence with the males was more through Abraham. Sarah did not have direct influence, though she had great respect from them. They appreciated her role with Abraham and her importance to Abraham, and so they treated her with importance as well.

Chapter Eight

JOURNEY TO CANAAN

#6 Recording 3:40 *Abraham Leaving Ur*

DR: Let's begin with the Abraham story: From Abram (his name at this point in the story) leaving the city of Ur, and why he left.

DS: When we move to that time space, there is purposefulness, as he prepared for his journey. There is some disagreement within him about the journey. But there is a sense of him feeling compelled to the journey. This one was very connected through his prayer space and his faith was unyielding. They were questions in him of his own faith, but he expected answers would come to his questions.

He put the journey off twice before deciding it could not be put off again. It's why the compelling feels strong within him. It feels as if he considers bringing others with him and is conflicted about that. Should he go alone? Who should come? These are some of his questions. The decisions of who to bring and who to stay weighed heavy on him. He was clear in leaving, clear in the journey, but not clear in some of the details of it.

He prayed on this and then trusted God to show him. There was some trepidation that God would not show him, because there were two false starts. He had not left in the moment he thought he should have and so there was some act of contrition, forgiveness within him with God now that he was actually leaving.

It does not feel like there was danger where he was leaving from. There is a sense that he did not know why he was leaving. Later, he understood it better. But in the moment, it was an act of faith.

There were more people coming than at first he thought. First, through his prayers, he thought it would be a pilgrimage for himself. But when he put it off the first time, things shifted and changed. And when he put it off the second time, the urgency increased, and the details of it shifted and changed. It was as if there was a dance between him, his God, and his free will.

I do not have a sense of his destination or even his direction. But as I witness his preparations in leaving, there is a solemness in him. There was also the question of if he would return, when he would return, and a knowing that he would not. This truly was an act of faith on his part. And he feared his faith was not strong enough, that he had argued with God about the leaving time, about who would come and when they would go. When this one did finally leave, there was a sense of confusion, some fear, but still determination to follow what he had seen. To do as he was told. It was not blind obedience, but there was an element of obedience that seemed to fuel his strength. And once on the road, everything within him softened. His connection to God seemed to strengthen, his belief seemed to deepen, and his faith seemed to grow.

There is a sense of followers with him. But some of them do not stay with him. Some of them leave off and others join. There is some sense of a pilgrimage for him, but at the same time there are followers.

He is not a teacher of the followers or a keeper of the followers. He is focused on a journey. It feels as if he does not have a map, except the map is of his heart and in his prayers. And the coincidences seem miraculous to him. His needs provided; the directions pointed. He feels well-cared for. There is no urgency. There is a sense of a pilgrimage, a trek. He is alone within himself even though there are followers coming and going.

DR: How many people came with him from Ur initially?

DS: There were discussions, arguments, fears. He decided not to choose who would come and who would stay. He simply decided he would leave and asked all those to pray to know if they were to leave as well.

He did not want the responsibility of choice for he was doubtful that he was clear as he was when he first had the vision. It feels as if there is a house full of people, his house, his space, ten, twelve. And the message spread that they were to pray, and if in their prayers, they saw themselves journeying, they were to leave with him the next day.

It feels as if there was ten, sixteen, and then twenty. But upon leaving, it went back down to sixteen, twelve, ten. And then it even went down to eight. But it feels as he journeyed others came from where he left and caught up. Others came from the hillsides. At times there was as many as twenty or thirty, but other times as few as six or eight.

It just feels like he was not of concern of the followers. As if he left the followers in God's hands. He left it to the followers to choose who was to come, who was to go, who was to stay, who was to journey. It felt like a protection to him to leave this between them and their God. He felt uncertain to choose and afraid to choose.

#6 Recording 15:15 *Sarah Leaving Ur with Abraham*

DR: For his wife Sarah (named Sarai at this point in the Bible), what was her role and how did she feel about this whole journey?

DS: At first, she was to be left behind, and she would not accept that. But she struggled in joining. She wanted Abraham to tell her, and he would not.

At first, she did not follow, and then she did. It feels like she was always behind him, perhaps half a day, always questioning herself, questioning the route, questioning what Abraham was doing. She was not clear; she had doubts. She did not have the same skill of prayer that Abraham had. But she had knowing, and she decided to trust her knowing and she did follow.

She did not lead either. At some point they both were walking, guided by their own inner knowings. There was doubt when she followed. There was fear when she followed. *We are uncertain* …there's a sense of her wanting to turn back. There's a sense of her staying while he left. And there is a sense of her following and …*I cannot make sense of the sensations. There's such conflict within her. When I simply ask if she followed, I am told yes.* But there was a frustration in her following, not quite anger, but frustration. It was as if they, Abraham and Sarah, walked the same path, but not together. That they were each in their own understandings. Each in their own journey. Though they walked together from the outside, they walked singularly within.

It feels like the purpose of the journey was different for each of them, though I cannot tell you about the purpose in words. It was self-awareness. It was deepening of faith. It was strengthening connection. It was trust. It was questions and the exploration of questions. But it wasn't an easy path.

#6 Recording 19:06 *Abraham at Haran*

DR: The story of Abraham and his followers stopping at Haran and settling down there for a while, until Abraham's father's death. Can you explain that story?

DS: He was following his prayers, and each day he prayed to know if he was to continue. He had no destination. His followers grew and weakened. Then there was an illness among the followers. When they first stopped there, it was to care for the ones unwell. As much as he was in his own pilgrimage, it was not of his heart to ignore the followers, just not to be responsible for directing them.

Once there was a realization there was illness, they stopped to take care of those that were ill. That required harvesting of herbs and necessities for the illness. That led to more establishment. And in his prayers, he was looking for the day to leave and it did not come, and so the settlement grew.

Once the settlement settled and began to grow, and the illness left, he still prayed daily. But he did not ask about leaving any longer. There was a settledness here, and there was a calm within him. Joy might be too strong of a word, but a joy within him, and within Sarah. A camaraderie started to develop, because many of the followers were strangers to each other. The dynamic of a settlement grew on its own accord; friendships formed; family bonds found. And it came to a time where he only asked of God about movement once in thirty days. And at this point it feels as if Sarah would confirm. As if they, at this point confirmed each other's prayers and visions or perceptions. So, the settlement did not begin as a settlement but grew into one.

DR: Was his nephew, Lot, and his brother with him in Haran?

DS: One at a time please, the names?

DR: His nephew, Lot.

DS: Yes.

DR: And a brother?

DS: I want to say no. It feels more like the brother started and stopped, started, and stopped, and turned back. I want to say no to the brother. And so, it feels as if the brother followed, then turned back, followed, then turned back, three times, and regretted not following. The brother wanted to, but there were jealousies, pettiness, anger. The conflict within the brother is real and strong and has a childishness to it.

DR: How long were they in Haran? How many seasons?

DS: They went through a birthing season, human birthings. We would say seven seasons. There was consideration at five, but there were babies being born, not in the animals, but in the people. And there was a timing. All the pregnancies would be birthed by the beginning of the seventh season. They chose to wait for that. Though Abraham still prayed once a month, it was his decision to wait for the births to be completed.

#6 Recording 29:40 *Abraham's Family*

DS: It is why his father joined them, because his father knew of his voice, prayers, and encouraged it. It is why his father followed him. It is also why the brother did not.

#6 Recording 25:17 *Abraham's Family*

DR: Did Abraham and Sarah have any children during this time?

DS: Yes. I want to say two, but I'm not sure if it's two pregnancies or twins, but I want to say two.

DR: Are there names?

DS: I cannot access that. It feels like a male and a female, but I'm not certain.

DR: Do they survive and travel with Abraham when he left Haran?

DS: Yes, the boy was walking, but young. The girl, a babe in arms, but not strong. But Abraham had prayed for the day to leave and would not change the leaving day. Several of the children were weakened, not sick exactly, not an illness exactly, but not strong.

DR: So why did he finally leave? What prompted him?

DS: The prayers. He checked every month, every span, and again was directed to leave. They were a tribe, large, by the time they left.

DR: How large?

DS: Nine families plus Abraham's family. Each family with children. Some families with elders that were not of the family, but were adopted by the family.

#4 Recording 45:22 *Similar Tribes in the Vicinity*

DR: So, where Abraham and Sarah lived, in Canaan, were there other Hebrew tribes in the vicinity, similar tribes, similar beliefs?

DS: Yes, they were quietly discovered. They found each other through trading, through working. But these were quieter.

There was some status around Abraham that made some of the other families only very quietly friendly with them, as if they do not want to draw attention to themselves, and Abraham did draw attention.

They held similar beliefs for the most part. There were three generations. They were smaller families, but they had not come to what you would call a tribe yet. They feel as if they are small families that moved in this direction and then found a place to settle, were happy to find others of like mind, but did not band together. They wanted to be quiet in their life, simple in their lives, and it feels like there was never more than three generations in them.

DR: So where did these family groups come from?

DS: That is hard to say. It feels like there were five families, and they came from different directions. It doesn't feel like any of them knew each other when they arrived here. It feels like three of them had lived nomadically and had decided to settle, which brought them to the Canaan area. The other two had been in Canaan longer, perhaps for four generations, but there were still only three generations alive.

#4 Recording 47:49 *Abraham's Teachers in Canaan*

DR: What brought them, as well as Abraham and Sarah, what drew them all to Canaan?

DS: Growth, desire to know more, desire for experience. They were not missionaries in any way shape or form. It was about life experience; it was about life opportunities, and it was about learning. It feels as if there were educators or men of wisdom in Canaan and specifically for Abraham, he did seek out more learning and so sought to find elders wherever he heard of them.

DR: So, he heard that there were elders, teachers in the land of Canaan and so was drawn there?

DS: Yes. There were very positive experiences from his education meetings as a young man and as he grew and watched change in the families around him, he craved more wisdom. So, there were times he even spent time with elders that would not be called Hebrews, would not have the same faith, but had the experience of wisdom in life. So, he was not always quick to identify himself, but as a man of learning only.

DR: So, the elders who taught him in Ur, knew of these other teachers in Canaan?

DS: No. No. Abraham heard of them from travelers and there was concern because they were not always of the same beliefs. But Abraham was clever, and his intellect was recognized which is why he became known and stood out more than the other families would have liked. And so, he was respected for his intellect and discussions, philosophical discussions, faith discussions. He entered into even with those of different faiths, but he entered into them gently, without forthright zeal, but more to listen and to learn, and it increased his wisdom greatly.

Again here, Donna describes the visions she is seeing of Abraham in the circles of discussions. She can sense the challenge they presented to Abraham. She can feel the differences in faith and how that created discussions. She can also sense Abraham and how he embraced these differences in order to learn. Donna can feel the need within Abraham for "wisdom" not just knowledge. These responses are coming from a witness of these discussions and the feeling of Abraham as he grew within these circles. There is such a sense of the man Abraham did become, starting here.

DR: So, once he arrived in Canaan, Abraham sought out these wise men, these teachers?

DS: Yes. They had meetings. I don't know how to call them. They weren't classrooms. They weren't prayer services. They were meetings, discussions, where they discussed the way of living, the way of deciding, the class structures, the developments, and the implications of the developments. They were elders who had seen great change and discussed the events of those changes and the results of those changes. Abraham was of interest to this.

DR: What was the lineage of beliefs if they were different?

DS: I cannot see the lineage of the beliefs, but the main difference was in service to God and in that which is connected to what we would call the visions in prayer space. These men were not supportive of visions in prayer space. There was fear of that and so that was kept quiet by Abraham.

They had similar beliefs, but there was more strictness and more fear in them, but they were still supporters of simplicity. There was more fear about invention. There was more fear about the changes. It feels as if Abraham was more supportive of the changes. Abraham, although we are using the words of The Counsel, Abraham, he was more supportive of evolving, but Abraham would not call it evolving. These wise men in Canaan were not. So, the discussions were how to keep the life with honour, how to keep the life of simplicity. And, the strictness, they were far stricter, but they had seen things Abraham had not. They had witnessed invention and Abraham wanted to understand what the history had shown them and so he was a great listener of their stories. He only asked simple, pointed questions. He shared very little of his own experience and this catered to the ego of these men, and so they did not need to know of him. They liked the adorative place, that reverence, that Abraham had for their experience.

It does not feel like he did this for a long, long time. He did this with specific purpose and then, I don't know how, but then his presence there finished without them ever really realizing that the very things they were frightened of, Abraham practised, such as the visions in prayer space, the idea of talking to God.

DR: So, what happened to them and their beliefs? Did they disappear?

DS: No. Their beliefs hardened; their beliefs strengthened, and the fear strengthened as well. They became punishing, strict. It feels as if they also entered into the ruling of the city, as if there was somehow a connection between the rulers and these wise men; as if they somehow helped the rulers hold order. It wasn't clear the difference of state and religion. It was the wise men ruling the city. So, they became part of the rulers of the city, the organizers, those that kept the city organized and at peace.

#6 Recording 36:12 *Abraham in Egypt*

DR: The story of Abraham going down to Egypt with his family due to famine and then pretending that his wife was his sister, can you explain that story please?

DS: His faith was strong then and he could not be moved from what his prayers and visions showed him. He was directed that Sarah would be safer as his sister. She was not to show her strength or her power or her leadership. It feels as if, as his wife, she would be in danger. As if there was some type of practice to gift a wife, but he need not gift a sister. And so, he came to them as a widower, and it was well-believed because of his age.

This was an act of faith from his prayers for it was not an easy journey to Egypt. And there were many questions. Some of the tribe turned away, turned back, and he forgave them. He entered Egypt, not as a chieftain or king, but as the eldest of the tribe, respected for his years. It was very quiet. There was no sign of power, and so he was no threat.

Some welcomed them, found places for them. But after the arrival and the places were found, this was not how they thought it would be. They were not equals, and this was hard.

He prayed daily for guidance, and on the days he heard nothing, he knew he was to hold the course, stay the way. And on the days anything else was to change, he would know. He did not know why they were there; he just knew this was where they needed to be. And it wasn't until after events occurred that he understood.

Not all of the tribe were so easily trusting, but they did trust him. And so, when they could not trust God, they would trust him. And he was easier with this now. It did not bear weight on his shoulders as it had in the younger man, because he had full faith of his prayer.

At this stage of Abraham's life, I am in touch with the depth of his faith and also how he has grown into his leadership. There is a sense that he understands his place and has acceptance of that place. As we speak these words, I am within the spirit of Abraham and can feel his peace and his acceptance of his life. It feels to be more than maturity. It feels a faithful, deep acceptance of his place in the world and a trust that he will always be in his place. This faithful, deep acceptance enables Abraham to move through what is asked of him. The depth of his trust and faith is wonderful to sense and be with.

DR: Did he end up in the Egyptian court or help to serve the hierarchy?

DS: He was in their service; he was not given title or credit. His wisdom was recognized; his fairness was recognized. And so, a place was made for him, but without title. And he saw that this was good, and that he was making a difference. He accepted he did not have a need of title. But it was his age and his wisdom that got him this place.

DR: Then, he was more or less an advisor to the court?

DS: We can't agree to the word advisor. It feels more like a right-hand man to someone of power. It was very quiet. Abraham, you see, did not lie. And so, the titled one he worked with/for, did not ask questions, because he did not want to know answers. But he did trust the wisdom of Abraham. He did not want to know it came from the prayer, and so he did not ask, because Abraham would not lie. They knew this about this man (Abraham), that he was a truth sayer which made him useful and dangerous.

DR: Did he help directly, or did he guide them in civil or military or agricultural affairs?

DS: It was civil. He brought an element of compassion to decisions, and fairness to decisions. The one he worked with/for heard petitions. It was the place of problems solved, ownership decided, permissions granted. And Abraham softened the will of the deciding magistrate or whatever he was. Abraham softened those decisions with wisdom, not with softness but with a compassionate wisdom. His counsel made sense and that's why it was listened to.

DR: Is there a name for who he worked for or a title, or position? How high up?

DS: I want to say magistrate. It feels like one who judges, hears cases, solves conflicts. But it is among common folk; it doesn't feel like it's only the upper classes. It's more common folk. When I see such a place, I don't see robes and jewels. I see workers, farmers, common men, merchants, asking for fair decisions to things that cannot be decided among themselves. It does not feel that it's about crimes. But it is about decisions and sharing and land lines and products, grains and farm goods, animals, and stock.

#6 Recording 44:48 *Sarah in Egypt*

DR: Did Sarah have an active role or less active role when they were in Egypt?

DS: Sarah could not be active in Egypt. For her to be seen as the powerful, wise voice she was, would have been dangerous. They needed to be seen as a meek tribe, led by an old one. That's the position they assumed. Those who knew her, also knew her wisdom. But it was more known among the females than the males. Somehow, she would have been a threat to have any power or wisdom recognized any place but with the females. And so, her influence was strong among the females, but quiet.

#6 Recording 45:39 *Leaving Egypt*

DR: When and why did they finally leave?

DS: Something changed in the rulings, in the ruler, in the politics of the place, and the one that favored Abraham, was not favored by the new rulers. Questions were posed of Abraham and his families.

There were questions asked, and watchings, investigations, and suspicions. They stayed longer than some of them thought they should have. But the prayer did not say to leave, and so they did not go, at first. But then more changes occurred in the ruling classes, more conflict, more suspicions, more greed, more power struggles.

Sarah initiated the move through a dream, and then when Abraham took the dream to the prayer space, the instructions for leaving were provided.

The tone of the place changed. The peace of the place changed, and Abraham's influence could no longer be used, could no longer be felt. He no longer had a part to play. He had difficulty believing this, and that's why the dream first came through

Sarah and then it was confirmed to his prayers.

DR: Is there a name for the former ruler and/or new ruler of Egypt at that time?

DS: There was conflict between two powerful bases of power, two different bases of power, each with their own choice (of leader). *I cannot see the details.*

There was a squabble. *I'm not sure what I am seeing whether it is between two brothers or between the son of the king and the head of the army.* There were squabbles between two very powerful men, and it was about who was more powerful, whose influence went farther. It degraded into conflict. Foolish squabbles, foolish contests. It feels as if the leader at the time let it play out, as if it were between his son and the head of an army or another powerful man. And the one in charge decided to let it play out, so that the most powerful would win and take command. That was the mistake., That's what caused everything to deteriorate and divide. The tradition was abandoned in some way. *But I cannot see the details of the namings.*

DR: Was the former ruler who let this happen deposed or killed?

DS: He was resigned. He could see the two young bulls, but did not care to fight. And, he let it play out. He was poisoned by one of the young bulls because suspicion was so cautious, and distrust was so deep, that it was not believed that he would allow a winner to win. He was poisoned though it truly was unnecessary. He would have surrendered to the winner. He wanted the realm left in strength, and he wanted that strength proven.

DR: When Abraham and Sarah left, had they acquired wealth that they took with them?

DS: *The word wealth is not the right word.* They took what they needed. They had a little more than they needed, but they did not take wealth with them. They took what they felt would be useful for the journey, to help them get out of the city, out of the place and travel and establish again.

From the farmer's perspective, it would have been wealth. But from the higher levels, it would not have been called wealth. They had more than when they had arrived. But it was taken for use. It wasn't taken for pride or décor or power. It was taken for use, as if it could be sold, as if it could be bribes, as if it could ensure safety.

DR: Would this be livestock and food, grain, implements?

DS: There were chalices and things of metal and gold, but also the livestock. But that which would prove useful to get out of city, to get where they were going. It was more metallic. It was not coin, but it was that which could be sold, that which could be producing coin if needed.

DR: This was earned, not just given as a gift from the court?

DS: It was gifts. There were some rules about which of these articles could be bought and who could buy them. And so, the fact that they had them, gave them reputation, gave them someone's protection, because such a chalice or such a jug could not be bought by one of his caste. And so, if it was given to him, it was given with support and protection by the one who gave it to him. It represented someone's protection.

The livestock, the wealth in the necessities, was bought. That was allowed. But it feels like chalices, vases, jugs for wine could not be bought out of metal by them. They were only gifted. The fact they had them said something about who favoured them, and that provided a protection as they exited.

DR: When they exited, how many people came with them and where did they end up? In Canaan, the final destination?

DS: There is a lot of confusion at the leaving. It's like one whole group started to leave, but they got split off in the skirmishes, and conflicts. There were two smaller parties split off from the main party, who took another route. They left in piecemeal so as not to seem threatening in leaving in great numbers. As if one or two families together left, then three or four families left, and the one family and then another family.

They met outside where the skirmishers were. When they came to Canaan, they were one tribe. But they were perhaps halfway to Canaan before they were one whole tribe, before everyone was caught up.

It was safer for them to leave in families, in groups, smaller groups, because suspicion was everywhere. And again, the objects they had provided their protection, because it showed they were favoured. It didn't show who favoured them. It showed that they were favoured, because they could have such an object. And so, they were given a wider berth than had they not had those goods. Those goods were distributed among the families, so that everyone had something that showed them to be favoured. But they did leave in groups, and halfway to Canaan they came together, and it was safe to do so.

I can feel the danger and the careful scrutiny that they are all under. I can feel how Abraham's attitude, which he has maintained the whole of the time he was in Egypt, is one of non-threatening. He "keeps his head down". There is no pride or assertiveness to him. He is not protecting the people, because his deep faith knows that they are already protected by God. They are miraculously walking through danger and are not touched by it. I can literally feel the danger they walk through, untouched by it. Miraculous! I am so aware of how much the faith in Abraham leads them in this exit and how much that same faith seems to transpire down into the followers of the tribe. I can truly sense that they trust Abraham as much as they trust God.

DR: This fighting and skirmishing that happened early on, who was this with?

DS: It was about sides. Which nobles supported which side, with skirmishes between the sides. Nobles choosing which bull to support, hoping they were choosing the right one. And there was a lot of suspicions, a lot of looking for traitors, or betrayals. Suspicion. Choosing sides, making sure you're on the strongest side, changing sides. It was just mayhem, not so much battles, but just this confusion of who is loyal to whom, and who is favoured by whom. It was just mayhem.

DR: This was among the Egyptians, among the nobles?

DS: Yes, and it filtered into the cities, into those who worked for, who they worked for, and were they on the right side. And when it looked like one side was losing, then they would change sides. It feels like it was just mayhem.

DR: When they finally met up halfway back to Canaan, how

large was the group and where did they end up once they finished the journey?

DS: Near twice the number that arrived in Egypt, with some strong leadership, younger men, forty, fifty years old, strong leaders. It feels like there were three, but there was no division between them. They had witnessed Egypt and its descent into competition and power. Though there were three, almost like lieutenants, they were very cooperative and supportive. There were these three because it was easier for information to be relayed for understanding, for directions. Almost like three sub-chiefs. Abraham still led. Sarah, now, could lead as well. Feels like they were twice the number. There were three tribes, because there were three men that led, strong faithful men.

DR: Where did they end up when they finally settled?

DS: When we follow the journey, they have one stop, longer than they were expecting, and it is hard to get everyone going again. *Not sure what to tell you.* They head to Canaan. They have one stop, and then when they start again, they move more south, and they travel longer to the point that is long. And they move west, and not for long, and then they stop, and they settle. They were trying to find a place, but Abraham couldn't get clarity with the prayer. And so, they made a decision among the leaders and chose a place. It feels like they went south and then west. *But I am not certain. It feels like they traveled longer than they thought they would. That's the best I can give you.*

#6 Recording 30:37 *Abraham, The Sacrifice*

DR: The story of Abraham going to sacrifice his son Isaac. Can you explain the story?

DS: *Move me to the time frame now, please.*

There is strife within Abraham. He is afraid. He feels the responsibility of the tribe now and it makes him afraid to trust his prayers for so many. They all trust his prayers. So many, they all trust his prayers now, and not their own.

The story of Isaac was partially a test of his own faith; a test of his own creation. Feels as if he was challenging his God, negotiating with his God. He was frightened of the word of God. This all grew slowly within him, but it grew and led him to that day.

He is an old man now, and it is hard to remember the trust of the nine-year old boy he was. He never wanted the responsibility of the tribe. He only wanted to follow the word. And now everyone was following the word, but it was the word through him, not through themselves. And the weight of it made him afraid to trust the word he heard, to trust the prayer he knew, to trust the voice he heard.

I can feel his fear that has taken time to root and grow. I can feel how old he is and how far he feels from the faith of the nine-year-old boy he was.

It feels as if it is a test of his own making, as if he challenges, the word, the God. But if what he is hearing is truth, then God will stay his hand. It is not the way it was told.

It is like he threatened his God. He surrendered his fear. He surrendered his trust. And simply asked God to stay his hand if what he heard in his prayer was still truth, was still God.

There were only two witnesses, Sarah, and another man.

It was the other man that changed the story, because in the moments before Abraham's hand was stayed, there was almost a madness within him from the fear. And the other man did not want that madness known or told to anyone. And Sarah agreed that he could change the story.

I can then feel the concern of the man watching. I can feel this man's concern, even fear, at the madness Abraham expresses in this time. I can feel that this man cannot allow the others to perceive any weakness in Abraham and so the story must be changed.

I witness a simple glance between Sarah and this man, and with that glance an agreement made, with no words, to change the story as it is told to the others.

But Abraham's hand was stayed. It feels like it was something miraculous; like a bird landing on his hand or knocking the knife or landing on his shoulder, something miraculous. And he knew; and the fear fell from his eyes and the fear fell from his heart. And he knew the same feeling he'd known when he was that first time in prayer of nine years old.

And there was deep sorrow and great regret at his doubt. Then he did fall to his knees in prayer and gratitude.

<u>This was no sacrifice asked for from God.</u> It was a dare. It was Abraham asking for proof, and proof he was given.

Sarah understood from one glance, what this story could mean if it is told differently. There is no sense of a lie being told. The story is told to allow everyone to feel a weakness of their faith and the

194

renewal when the test is answered. The tribe needs the confidence they have in Abraham to remain strong. And, with this experience, Abraham truly is renewed and deserves the faith of the tribe. He is now ready to be the leader of this tribe again, now with the innocent faith of the nine-year-old he once was. Truly amazing!

Chapter Nine

ABRAHAM AND MELCHIZEDEK

And Melchizedek king of Salem brought out bread and wine: and he was [is] the priest of the most high God. And he blessed him, and said, "Blessed be Abram of God Most High, Creator of heaven and earth, and blessed be God Most High, which hath delivered your foes into your hand". And [Abram]gave him a tenth of everything. (Genesis 14:18-20)

#4 Recording 39:54 *Their Relationship*

DR: Can you explain the relationship between Abraham and Melchizedek?

DS: We want to say that Melchizedek began as a voice only Abraham understood and heard. First as a voice only Abraham heard, and then as a voice that only Abraham understood. Melchizedek was an attempt to help... from the council of light... and deliberately so, working only through one in the beginning. This was so that changes could be small, support could be small. And then watching the effects of it.

Then, Melchizedek became a being, more brethren type to Abraham and became more involved in the tribe itself. Melchizedek had god-like abilities, abilities that which would be perceived as god-like, because he did not get sick, he did not age, he did not need to eat much, he did not need to sleep much. Those differences were noted. And by this point there was jealousy on your planet. And that's when differences were noticed. Jealousy used observation to arm itself.

Melchizedek also healed quickly. Though he did not fight, he could defend. There was no offence in Melchizedek. There were teachings, information, and attempts to clarify things. This did create followers and those who did not follow. Melchizedek personally experienced the presence of fear on this planet. It was not something he had encountered in his personal experience before. Witnessing fear in some of the non-followers was an exercise of growth for himself. He did not hold fear; he was not infected by fear; but he witnessed fear. And it almost feels like this was a new experience. If not the first time, he hadn't witnessed it often. And to see it on the planet was disheartening. But the nature of EVOLUTION was truly how fear was born on the planet, because there was much the men could not control, that the Earth controlled. And the lack of control was the breeding ground for the fear.

#4 Recording 44:41 *Melchizedek Speaking to Abraham*

DR: Would you say he spoke to Abraham before he incarnated on Earth?

DS: It feels as if there was a voice that Abraham heard that only after Melchizedek arrived that he recognized as Melchizedek. Prior to that it was God; it was guidance.

#6 Recording 28:51 *Abraham and Melchizedek*

DR: Was Melchizedek talking to him and he thought this was God? Did he pray?

DS: No, it was God! The God he knew. It was God. It was the same voice he had always heard. He heard him first as a boy – eight, nine years old. And there was a recognition he knew in his bones. It was the God he knew.

#4 Recording 45:07 *Melchizedek as Mentor*

DR: When the Bible says God spoke to Abraham, this was...

DS: Melchizedek, yes.

DR: And Melchizedek was his mentor, his teacher?

DS: Yes.

#4 Recording 45:20 *Melchizedek's Role*

DR: And was Melchizedek's mission to enable Abraham to begin a new religious theme?

DS: The intent of Melchizedek was to help, to teach, to help mankind remember what was forgotten. But it was only after he incarnated did he realize the intricacies of memory. And perhaps the memories he wanted all to remember were too buried, and so the teachings arose. The theory was that when you teach, the truth of the teachings awakens the memories. And that is how truth is strengthened. Because you all have memories and when you hear truth, memories awaken, and you know truth because memories and truth align. So yes, though he did not come to create such, it was the mechanism that needed to be used, because the memories were inaccessible without that.

#4 Recording 46:52 *Abraham and Melchizedek*

DR: Did Melchizedek develop a belief system for Abraham to then utilize or did Abraham develop a belief system with commandments and rules?

DS: Melchizedek activated as best he could the memories in Abraham. Abraham allowed his memories to work with his knowings of the present moment to create the teachings. Melchizedek was involved, but once the memories in Abraham were awakened, the truth did not need support. And once the truth was awakened, then Abraham could see how, perhaps, others' memories could be awoken. Though it was Abraham who did the creating, it was with Melchizedek's support.

#4 Recording 48:05 *Abraham and Melchizedek*

DS: But once Abraham's memories were awakened, Melchizedek was not as needed, as if that was the achievement. Not an expected achievement, but an achievement. It proved the memories could be woken. And now it was time to discover how to awaken more memories in the minds of men, of mankind, of humans.

#4 Recording 1:10:22 *Melchizedek's Appearance*

DR: When you say you asked about Melchizedek and then you saw an image...

DS: Yes, I saw Melchizedek.

DR: That was unique.

DS: *He was a unique being. When he came down, he took a humanoid form that was very muscular. The upper body was like a Schwarzenegger – muscular, but his arms almost had a sense of wings to them. And there were marks on him. I don't know if there was a texture of skin or a tattoo. I don't know what they were, but there were marks on his skin. And when he came down, really, I got to tell you (laughing), it was like he jumped out of a plane, out of something, and landed on his two feet. You know, like a superhero. And he was much bigger up top than below, but he did have two legs and he was very muscular. I don't know what clothes he had on, because there wasn't a sense of clothing. There was a sense of texture on his skin. There was a sense of markings. There was a sense of a head with dark hair. There was a sense of strong jaw. If he was a man, he was a very large man. Like he would have been like 8 or 10 feet tall and took up a lot of space. He was very tall. Fascinating.*

Discussion

ABRAHAM AND SARAH

#6 Recording 1:03:56 *The Followers of Abraham*

DS: This session was different for me because I actually went to where the answer to the question was. I read Abraham. I read Sarah. I read the situation that was present to the timeframe and traveled with them. I saw inside their hearts, inside their being. I could feel the strength of Abraham's faith and the conflict when it came into jeopardy, into the challenge to God over his son, Isaac.

Abraham needed a sign. He needed a sign, because of what

he was losing. He found he was afraid he was losing faith. There was a feeling he had when he was nine years old, and he had lost that feeling. Because he really thought, *I am perfectly willing to be wrong here,* he really didn't want to be a leader of men. He wanted to be a man of God. And so, when the first journey began, he said to the others, "No, my prayers have sent me; follow your own prayers". And so people came, people went, people joined, people left, and, *again, I am perfectly willing to be wrong,* it felt like his father followed Abraham, because he knew his son, and he knew about his son's prayers.

It was like there was some type of competition, pettiness with the brother. His brother knew he could trust the prayers of Abraham, but he didn't want to trust the prayers and join in. And he regretted that decision. He changed his mind. He went; he followed and then he turned around. He followed again, then turned around again, and then never followed again. He regretted that to the day he died. He always regretted that. Abraham's brother knew that it was the wrong decision and that he had made it out of pettiness.

Abraham didn't want to be a leader, he just wanted to be the follower of his prayers. When he served in Egypt, it seemed to the Egyptians he had a natural wisdom. And because he was very old, they just attributed that to his age. No one wanted to know any more about it, because that would have put Abraham in danger. So, the Egyptians just didn't want to know.

#6 Recording 1:06:12 *Egyptian Power Struggle*

DS: In Egypt, it just felt like there were these petty squabbles over power. And the king at the time, if I can call him that, made it all into a game, without realizing how dangerous a game it would become. This game created division all the way down into the city and even among the servants as well as the nobles. And it all just disintegrated. It just changed the whole place, because it was a power struggle, and it broke with tradition.

It was like, "Okay, the strongest one gets to rule. Who's the strongest?" And so, they had battles and they had betrayals. It really degraded very, very, quickly. And the King of it all was poisoned. It was unnecessary, but everyone had become so suspicious that no one believed the King would accept the one who won it all. That's why he was poisoned. But he would have accepted the winner, because he thought of it as a game. It's very sad. He thought it was funny, and it was so destructive. He wanted to see what would happen when two powerful people were fighting to see who was the most powerful.

#6 Recording 1:07:38 *Objects of Protection*

DS: I could see that the tribe had some objects, like chalices or jugs for wine, or trays, and it was known that they wouldn't be allowed to buy those things. If they had them, it meant someone had favoured them. And that made those of the tribe safe, and Egyptian people gave them a wider berth. They didn't know who had given them these gifts, but just the fact that they had them, and because they didn't know who gave them to them, was enough. They didn't want to be on the wrong side come the end of the battles.

And it felt like the tribe split up when they left, like they didn't leave in one drove. It felt like it was safer this way. It was safer to get out, to leave, in families, and then gather later. And I did feel when they came into Canaan, there were three strong men that were like the next level down from Abraham. Almost like there were three tribes in one tribe now, or three clans, and each was head of their family? Tribe? Clan? They had witnessed the destruction of the power struggle in Egypt. There was much more cooperation among them because of that history, because of what they witnessed. That sort of kept their own egos in check. Fascinating.

#6 Recording 1:09:00 *Sarah Sister/Wife*

DS: It was safer if Sarah was thought of as Abraham's sister. It felt like his wife could be taken from him, or he should gift his wife, but his sister was safer. And she certainly couldn't be a powerful voice. Those who knew Sarah, among the females, knew who and what she was, but that wasn't common knowledge. It wouldn't have been safe. It wouldn't have been safe at all. They were coming in meekly, because that's the nature. They had to be seen that way. They couldn't be seen as a tribe; they couldn't be seen as a threat. Once the squabbles among the Egyptians about who would rule next began, the tribe's people had to be very, very meek. You didn't want to be thought of as harnessing any power or being any group with power. Fascinating.

#6 Recording 1:09:54 *Abraham's Prayers*

DR: Abraham as a young boy of nine, you said, talked directly to God?

DS: Yes, he called it his prayers.

DR: And then, I am trying to understand, because in an earlier recording you talked about him hearing the voice of

Melchizedek.

DS: Yes, that did happen. But it wasn't in the prayers, it was something else. It was like God sent Melchizedek as well. But his prayer connection was to God. I could see that Melchizedek was an influence, but that wasn't the only influence. That wasn't the final say. That was like a messenger from God.

DR: Okay, but you could see that influence in the session today?

DS: Yes, I could see the position of Melchizedek, but Abraham still took his first lead from what he called his prayer time. That's where Abraham would see his visions, or he would ask for guidance. And then, at times, God would send Melchizedek. I didn't see when. We have to explore that; I didn't see when or under what circumstances Melchizedek came about or why. But when you mentioned Melchizedek, I could see him, but he was second to the prayer voice, to that voice of God in prayer. He was more like a messenger.

#6 Recording 1:11:40 *Trouble Getting Names*

DR: It seems hard for you to get names.

DS: That's me. Every now and again it's like "Good Lord, I'm not that good". That's actually my fault. I'm not that good. You see, I don't know the Bible, and this is a good thing. I would be picking a name out of the air and my fear of getting it wrong gets in my way. That is a place where I have to grow. Because my fear of being wrong just can't even let me try.

DR: Wow, because that would be so cool to be able to tie in an

Egyptian ruler to Abraham's sojourn in Egypt.

DS: Well, the only other thing we could do is you could give me three or four names, and from the vibration of the name, I could pick the one that feels like the right vibration. We could do it that way.

#6 Recording 1:12:51 *Children of Abraham and Sarah during Journey*

DR: Abraham and Sarah had children when they were stopped in Haran, and these are not mentioned in the Bible.

DS: Yes, when you asked how long they stayed, I heard counting time through the birthing seasons. I immediately thought it was animals, and then I knew that it wasn't animals. It was like there was a number of pregnant women and mysteriously, all the pregnancies finished around the same time. And then, there were no other pregnancies. That's when they decided to leave. It wasn't hundreds of babies. There might have been fifteen, a dozen. I could see all these pregnant women, and then once the births were complete, that's when they left, and there were no other pregnancies.

DR: They had to travel with young children, infants?

DS: Yes, and some of them were sickly.

#6 Recording 1:13:48 *Numbers Leaving Egypt*

DR: Did you get a sense of when they left Egypt? You said, they were twice the number of when they entered. Was there a sense of what the number was roughly?

DS: No. I can see the tribe arrive, and then I can see the tribe leave. It's like they take up twice as much space when I see them. I'm just seeing a crowd. I see a crowd arrive, and then I see a crowd, twice the size, leaving.

At some point you asked about a number, how many families or something. It was like I went to the circle, and then I could count the families. I could see the family designations and that's how I counted them. But when you asked about arriving and leaving, it was just a crowd. I did not see the family designations. It was just a crowd of people arriving and then a larger crowd of people leaving. But they left in smaller numbers. They didn't leave as one crowd.

DR: There was fear of them being pursued when they left Egypt?

DS: Yes. Well, not pursued, as much as it would just look suspicious if hundreds of people left. But if families left, that wasn't suspicious, because families were leaving anyway. And so when we gave you those numbers, there were elders that weren't of the family, but had joined the family to leave. There were people that joined on the way to Egypt and there were people that followed that weren't from where Abraham started. There were people that joined and some of them were elders, and so they would be thought of as grandmothers and grandfathers with a family, but they weren't connected to the family. They had been adopted by the family. There was that sense of three generations, even though some of them weren't blood. There was a strong sense of generations in the families.

DR: Any sense of how long they were in Egypt?

DS: I don't know.

#6 Recording 1:16:09 *Traveling Back to Canaan*

DR: When they got back to Canaan were there people of their kind, their tribe?

DS: I didn't see the arrival in Canaan. I saw the journey. Felt like they paused, and then they went south, and then they went west. And I didn't really see them settle. I didn't see what was around them. I was more looking for direction. I didn't see the settlement, I just saw the stop of the journey.

#6 Recording 1:16:51 *Crossing the Red Sea*

DR: How did they cross the Red Sea? How did they move across the water?

DS: I didn't see that part, so I don't know. I didn't see the journey that close; it was almost like I was seeing it from a higher perspective, the movement.

DR: Well, there's a lot of new stuff there, and actually not what I expected. Pretty amazing. Some of the key biblical questions about the sister-wife thing were answered.

DS: Yes, it was for her safety. It was almost a sense that they could take your wife, or you gifted a wife, but not his sister. He needed to be perceived as this widower, this wise old man, because then he was no threat. They didn't need to be meek; they just needed not to pose a threat. They needed not to come across as powerful, interesting, but not powerful. And Abraham was such a faithful man.

#6 Recording 1:18:28 *Beliefs of the People Leaving Egypt*

DR: When the tribe left Egypt, these were people of deep faith at this point, bonded together in deep faith? It wasn't as if he had to teach them some truths? They were embedded with truths, right?

DS: It felt like it. It felt like the ones that followed Abraham and stayed with him were faithful people. And it was their faith that bonded them. He never nurtured them to have faith in him. He never, ever did that. That's why he shared responsibility of leader, because he didn't want the faith to be in him. At certain points it started to be faith in him, and he didn't like that.

He wanted them all in their own faith. He was a very faithful man, very much a servant of God. He didn't want to be seen as a representative of God. And at certain times, Abraham was seen that way, because his prayers were so clear and his direction so clear. But that's not how he wanted to be perceived. I think as Abraham got older, he got accustomed to it. He understood it more as his compassion and his understandings of people grew. He could accept it, but he still was always pushing them to have their own connections to God, and that he wasn't their connection to God.

Abraham made his decisions from his prayers, but he didn't make their decisions. In the very first journey, he was adamant. He was not going to choose who was coming and who was staying. They had to pray and find truths for themselves, because he didn't want that responsibility.

Abraham wasn't looking to be a leader. He was just looking

to follow the word of God and at first, he didn't. He argued with God. Then when he finally left, he was afraid, because he hadn't left when he was told to.

Once Abraham was in the journey, his connections were more solid again, because he stopped fighting with God. But he never wanted to be a leader of men, as I perceived him.

Abraham felt he was doing what was right. "If you pray and you see the same thing, then we will go together". But he didn't invite or choose or select.

Even the three men I saw that were sort of like the second level of command coming out of Egypt, Abraham didn't choose them. It was more like they were just natural leaders. These were men people could follow, and these were men people trusted. They were also faithful men.

What they witnessed in Egypt was exactly opposite to what they were, and it reminded them to stay that way. It really did, because the original way of being wasn't power conflicts and it wasn't competition. It was a shared supportedness, and they had that, but **it was more focused on their faith in the God and being led by God, as opposed to a man.** And it just felt to me like Abraham really fought against being God's representative to them.

Section Five

JOSEPH - JEALOUSY AND DEATH

The story of Joseph starts with the interaction between him and his brothers. *At seventeen years of age, Joseph tended the flocks with his brothers, as a helper to the sons of his father's wives, Bilhah and Zilpah, and Joseph brought back bad reports of them to their father.* (Genesis 37:2)

They saw him from afar, and before he came close to them, they conspired to kill him. They said to one another, "Here comes that dreamer!" Come now, let us kill him and throw him into one of the pits; and we can say, "A wild beast devoured him". We shall see what comes of his dreams. (Genesis 37:18-21).

So begins the long complex saga of Joseph, rising from slavery to holding a most powerful position in the Egyptian court, and eventually reconciling with his brothers after putting them through deserved agony.

The story is one of overcoming huge obstacles along the way to power and influence. It could be true as is, but seems far-fetched to be able to rise so far up from humble beginnings as both a slave and a foreigner. His rise was accomplished solely due to his dream interpretation abilities. But the Pharaoh also had many advisors, magicians, and wise men who could also interpret dreams. According to the Bible story, *they all failed to do so* (Genesis 41:8), leaving it to Joseph alone to come to the rescue, and make a name for himself with the Pharaoh.

With this story, I was curious about the near killing of Joseph by his brothers, the gift of his ability to correctly interpret dreams, and how he was actually able to rise so high in the Egyptian hierarchy. An interesting side puzzle to this story is why Jacob blessed Joseph's two sons, Ephraim and Manasseh, and elevated these two grandsons to the same status as Jacob's sons.

#7 Recording 3:46 *Joseph, Son of Jacob*

DR: Let's start with the biblical story of Joseph, son of Jacob, his whole story, his sojourn in Egypt, and his rise.

DS: This was an interesting time. The Counsel was, once again, paying attention, as if they had left attention on the Earth for a while, and at this stage of evolution returned their focus to the planet.

There is an admiration around this name, Joseph, for the changes he made with the steadfastness he exhibited. It feels as if he was the first in a line of the humans that really came into an authority within themselves. He was faithful to his God; he was supported by that religion. But there was an inner authority within him. This is what brought the Counsel's attention back.

We started to see the development of inner authority in the humans. He was the first in his tribe to come to this. It wasn't bestowed upon him; it came from an inner place.

This one had a sense of directedness within him. There was a strong connection as a boy to the ways of his tribe and his family. And when we are within this one as a boy, his faith is strong.

But there is also something else in him that was there even at the age of eight or nine, a strength, an inner strength, righteousness, a determination. He wanted to, not be a leader of men, but still make a difference. He was a man of his word. He wanted to be a man of his word even as a boy.

He watched the men around him and he could see through them. He knew who was of honour and who was not. He decided around the age of eight or nine that he would be a man of honour. That held in his heart as he grew through the stages of his manhood. And so, honour was important, integrity, the honour of your word. But there was also this faithfulness to his God, to his beliefs. We are going to say at a certain stage of his journey, he did struggle to find a balance between being an honourable man, and still in strength, and also faithful. He struggled with that, as if in being faithful to his God, he did not feel in the strength of his manhood. He wasn't sure how to relate the two.

There were several times in his life he felt tested by his God. But what was really being tested was his integrity and the depth of his belief, where the line for sacrifice could come. He felt very aware at each testing. He also felt that he had made the right choices.

What was the name of the other man you were asking about?

DR: His father, Jacob.

DS: He had witnessed compromises made by Jacob, and though he did not judge his father for it, he did not want to follow in his footsteps that way. He was a bit more black and white. When his father showed the grey areas, he struggled with that. "Compromise" his father called it. He struggled with compromise. But as Joseph came into his manhood, there was a black and whiteness to him. It was respected by those around him, because it made him very clear. It also made him predictable. But the other men liked to work with him, because he did what he said, and he meant what he said. But there was not a lot of compromise. He had not yet discovered compassion.

When we see Joseph, we see him in black and white, with little compassion, with his integrity and honour, the respect for him growing, his reputation growing. And his disdain sometimes grew as well. He did not have compassion for those who created a grey area, who could compromise their faith or integrity. And it feels to us that this brought him much work, much respect, and admiration. But even with this, it feels as if he was careful about this. The admiration was for the work, not for him.

There was an inner authority within Joseph. He had an, *not impervious, that word would be too strong,* but he had an ability to rebuff other people's opinions. As long as he was in his integrity and his space, he did not listen to others. And there was a point in the family where this created problems.

The other brothers, like the father, found grey areas to compromise. Joseph would not; he could not. And there was some disdain. He prayed about it. There were judgments against his brothers, not against his father. Somehow, he managed to allow father's compromise. But with the brothers there was disdain. The brothers felt themselves being measured to him, and they didn't like the measuring stick.

There was conflict there. It feels as if Joseph did encounter situations in his life, in the full manhood, when he started to better understand compassion. He felt the Lord was trying to show him compassion. He did not understand it, but he did try with those of less fortune, those of less means.

Joseph could not compromise, but he did start to get a sense of what compassion was. And it started to change him, soften him. He still could not see the grey area, but he could soften around the terms of his right and wrong behaviours, of the measurement of right and wrong behaviour. But it feels as if it was too little too late for the breach in the family.

There was jealousy, competitiveness, disdain, comparisons. It stirred the pot with the brothers, and it created competition between them. Joseph often was the winner in the competitions for work, for respect, for attention. Though he was very careful to put the attention to his work, the brothers did not see it this way. And it was as if the brothers, two in particular, were tired of hearing the praises of Joseph, and it started to create animosity.

As we explore the family and family relationships, the insight into Joseph within himself and then within his family is very clear to me. I can feel Joseph as he feels guided to explore compassion and I can feel his confusion as he does not understand the lesson of compassion.

Then my focus is shifted outwards to those who relate to Joseph in his work, and I can feel, deeply, the admiration and respect Joseph receives.

Then my focus moves to the family. I can feel the love and acceptance Joseph has of his father, but when my focus is shifted to the brothers, that acceptance disappears. Joseph feels much more demanding of his brothers, much more judging of them. I can feel in the energy emanating from the brothers, that they see this as arrogance. It is not arrogance, as I feel it. It is a form of dedication to how Joseph lives and does his work. He is unyielding in his dedication. The brothers do not see Joseph as he is. From the outside looking in, they perceive Joseph very differently, and I can feel that they see Joseph through their jealousy, through their hurt. It is fascinating to experience this emotion in the brothers and see how it clouds the way they see Joseph.

The last blows were around either an illness with the father or the death of the father. As if the father started to show favouritism to Joseph, and that feels like the last straw. At the father's death, something snapped. This is where the brothers decided to bring him down a notch or two. There were high emotions, animosity, and pride. Joseph could see this in his brothers, and he thought of each of these qualities as a sin and made the mistake of saying so.

Joseph took pride in his work, but he did his best not to take pride in himself. There was this really interesting connection between his work and his faith; his honour and his faith. Each good deed or each good creation he made, that he was involved with, he gave the credit to the Lord working through him.

This seemed to heighten animosity in the family for now the brothers heard that he was the hand of God, which is not what he meant. He just was doing his best not to take pride in the work himself but being the vehicle for the work.

He was so precise in his articulations and his meaning. And he meant what he said, but still people praised <u>him</u>, and still <u>he</u> was given more respect. And the brothers could have no more of it.

There was no murderous intent. It was to teach a lesson, to bring him down a notch or two; to see if the hand of God would save him, stop them from hurting him. It started, as odd as it sounds, with prayer, with them putting him to his knees and treating him as if he was the hand of God, ridiculing it. There was confusion in Joseph. He could not make them see. He could see their pride, their jealousy, their competition, and he made the mistake of calling them on these sins and that pushed the situation to its limit.

We are going to suggest that the strength of inner authority was still present in Joseph. The faith in his God was still present with him and there was an aspect of surrender to him, within him. As if he was accepting their punishment even though he did not believe he deserved it. There was a sense of surrender to it, and this seemed to heighten the situation even more, because he would not respond. He would not fight back. And there was a blow struck, almost accidentally, and the blow created the murderous intent, the death.

I can feel the surrender within Joseph. I can feel how he uses his faith to interpret what is happening and how he surrenders to it. I can feel that his surrender is to the will of his God, not his brothers. I can feel how hurt Joseph is in his surrender. Then, I can feel the brothers and how they are lost in their emotions. I can feel the absence of murderous intent. Instead, I can feel the brothers are frustrated, misunderstood, hurt, jealous – all of these emotions are stirred together, and reactions lead to actions, but actions without thought or control.

Do not mistake our words. The brothers were in blind anger, but never was the intent to actually murder him; just to make him bend a little, to make him see himself through their eyes. And they did not succeed.

There was horror at what they had done, and fear, and shame. And there was great confusion over what to do now, and how to do it. There was enough integrity and faithfulness in them not to leave him, though that was the first idea. But it doesn't feel like they left him.

They brought him back with a story of a fall. It was, not the destruction of the family, but it created severances between the brothers, distance between them. And it was always left unexplained. Others who watched, attributed it to grief. Those closer knew something else was wrong. Those very close had suspicions.

#7 Recording 22:07 *The Counsel's View*

DS: *It was also the beginning of something else. Because there is this sense of the Counsel's watching with great interest.*

A loss of control, not that it never happened before, but with these men they had never experienced it. For these brothers, the loss of control was something they danced with and fought with the rest of their lives. As if they felt something take them over, and it made them very afraid of what could cause them to be so blind with their pride and their anger.

It was interpreted by those who spoke with them that it was of the devil, and in their small understandings perhaps it was the best explanation. But as the Counsel watched, the Counsel witnessed the growth of something, and this is what kept their interest to the Earth, because they had not witnessed this before.

At the time there was no word for this. It wasn't about the violence for the Counsel. It was the impetus. It was the motivation that they found fascinating, curious. And that it only was lifted once the man was dead. There was complete blindness to what they could cause, what could result, and only once the result occurred, did the blindness lift. It was an active moment for an instinctive, dark retaliation. *I struggle to give you words because at its initiation there were not words and as I look through the Counsel's eyes, they were without words.* But they watched with fascination as this act, even though it wasn't everyone that wielded the stone that killed. This act was as if everyone had done it, and the Counsel witnessed each brother dance with and struggle and be partially damaged by what had occurred. In each brother, a compensating behaviour was different. This is what held the Counsel's interest, how each handled it differently. And yet there was within them now, a righteousness to their behaviour, a defence of it, and still an ignorance and a denial of the blindness that had occurred.

This was a demonstration to the Counsel of a whole other level of growth in the humans. It was tied to their emotional responses, and how the emotional responses could yield behaviour. Not because this had never happened before, but it had never been witnessed by the Counsel, and the depth of it and the power of it, and then the justification of it. This is when the Counsel recognized how far man had evolved in its consciousness and saw what a great difference this consciousness was from the original seed of Adam.

The Counsel had intended from our beginnings to allow the consciousness that they implanted within Adam and Eve in our world, to evolve in its own natural course. They were determined not to interfere in that natural evolution. It was Joseph and all that he was that brought the Counsel's attention back to the Earth.

I can sense that the Counsel's interest returned because of the vibration that Joseph's dedication to his God, Joseph's inner authority created. The Counsel is fascinated by how this violence took place. The level of emotion that is created in the animosity of the brother, the blindness in reaction to that level of emotion. There is a sense of the scientist witnessing an amazing discovery, as the Counsel witnesses and sees the aftermath of the actions. I can even sense the Counsel's fascination extending to the compensating behaviours that are later created differently within each brother.

#7 Recording 27:10 *The Family After Joseph's Death*

DS: From that moment, the family didn't separate, but there was distance that was never recovered. There was small blame, as each wanted to recognize that they hadn't done it, and yet <u>they</u> had. Now, this was in the way of the family, and it actually, we are going to suggest, was passed down to the next generation, because there was some animosity between the brothers that their sons continued. And it took nearly three generations for that animosity to be peacefully resolved. The story was never told, so there was no understanding of the source of the animosity. And yet, if this father disliked that father, then this son must dislike that son, then this grandson must do the same. Feels like it was three generations before questions were asked and peace was brought to the animosity.

When this event happened, it wove a thread into the consciousness of the tribe. And even when the animosity was peacefully resolved, the thread was still there. It introduced something. This is why it was written about. It is why it caught the attention of the Counsel. Not because this type of thing had never happened before, but it had never happened this way in this tribe, with such ferocity and then defended.

#7 Recording 44:02 *Death of Joseph, Son of Jacob*

DR: Joseph was killed by his brothers after his father Jacob's death?

DS: It feels like there was an illness with the father. I believe the father died. But it was around this time, because the father favoured Joseph in his illness or at his deathbed. *I am not sure which.*

He wanted to see Joseph first, alone, without the others. And again, the inequality of that was like the last straw. Joseph was now obviously the favourite. The father was close to death and he wanted to see Joseph and asked the others to leave the room. And that was the last straw, for Joseph to be favoured in the village, in the tribe, and now be favoured in the family. It was the last straw.

#7 Recording 29:08 *Joseph Sold into Slavery*

DR: The story of Joseph being sold into slavery, going into Egypt, and then rising in power in Egypt, did this happen or not?

DS: I do not see the travel to Egypt. I do not see the simple man. I see him raised; I see him respected. I do not see him as powered.

Creator of All That Is, show me the timeline. I'm uncertain around this.

I am not seeing what you described to Egypt. I'm seeing a much simpler story that had deep impact on the family and on the tribe. I am not seeing him sold. What is the connection then to Egypt, the story of power? *Creator of All That Is, can we see the true story of this place?*

It feels like it is a different man. It feels like it is a man who is similar to Joseph in integrity and dedication, but I am not understanding how the two stories come together or connection. I would not say that this story of Joseph in Egypt is fiction, but it does not feel like it is the Joseph of Jacob.

It is either fiction, or it is another Joseph. Because I'm not seeing a link between the two. When I check the brothers, I am not seeing a brother who went off in this way. I do not have an answer to that, I do not see it as that way.

#7 Recording 33:06 *Joseph of Egypt*

DR: The person who you see in Egypt, the other Joseph, was he a Hebrew and can you tell a bit about his story?

DS: His name is also Joseph. *Is that his name?*

We see another man of great dedication, but this one has a mission, to make changes. This one is a little bit more of a zealot. He feels he is doing God's work, feels he is led by God, that he hears God's voice. But about thirty percent of the time, it is not the voice of God. It is as if he is inspired by God force, and then his mind decides how to enact God's will.

He is dedicated to his God. There is integrity and he means well. But it feels as if there is a little bit more hardness to his black and white. He is similar in nature to the Joseph we just spoke of earlier, but there is a difference here. This one has pride in his connection to the God. This one has pride in being chosen to do God's work. And so, this one is not as dedicated if we would compare him to the other Joseph. This one does seek power where Joseph did not. But this one justifies his seeking of power, in that with the power, he can do more of God's work. And in the beginning, he really did use the power that way. It gave him influence. He was able to undo things, change contracts, change things for the betterment. But it does feel like he was also somewhat seduced by the power.

It's the same thread we saw in the brothers with Joseph. It's like a thread of a different colour, a more negative nature. This thread can still have the voice of righteousness and a sound defence for action. But there is something negative in it.

In the story of the other Joseph of Egypt, I find a thread of a different colour. When I open to sense it more deeply, I can feel the nature of this thread and its nature is behavioural. It feels to me that this new dance with power is not something that we have encountered before in the time of this Joseph story line. It has an ability to seduce, and so in the beginning, his power was used for the betterment of the people, but then it changes. I can sense the seduction and how that seduction succeeds. This feels new to the story. This feels like something being born on the planet and growing, not just in this man, but in others. We witnessed it out of control in the Abraham story among the powers of Egypt. It is interesting to me to feel this influence growing into power and then feel the seduction of that power grow into selfishness. Fascinating.

#7 Recording 36:39 *Influence of Power*

DS: In that time, they would call it the influence of the devil. It wasn't. It was the growth of something in the personality and the evolution of man at that time. But in this one, the thread was stronger. The seduction of power and the pride itself was fed by this. If we studied others of this era, we would find this thread almost everywhere.

As we said earlier, it's what brought the Counsel's attention back. Something had grown, something had seeded itself in the personality, the psychology, of the humans. But it was in this one as well. It feels like it was in all humans, but there were those who were able to manage it and those that were not.

It feels like this one we are seeing coming to power in Egypt did succumb to this seduction of power. For the most part, we would say near eighty percent of the time, this one did as he intended. He influenced contracts. He influenced judgments, punishments. But he was also enamored with the power itself, and the influence, and sometimes his selfishness. That's how it came in ... sometimes his selfishness would allow the seduction of the power. And it was selfishness that allowed this thread of a more negative nature to grow.

Equality was starting to be sacrificed. It was what was sacrificed in the family of Joseph (son of Jacob). The brothers did not feel equal. It was not Joseph's intention to become greater than his brothers. But that is how it was perceived. That one was better than the others. He could not be better than them; he came from same stock.

Here, as well in Egypt, we see this same thread. And it feels like equality suffers. As if this one (Joseph of Egypt), doing his best to look after his people, started to see the inequalities and started to be personally affected by them. Particularly when, with the power, he became above those he thought himself equal to. He lost the internal battle to stay equal to those he was fighting for, and was seduced by the power. He still did good eighty percent of the time, but selfishness came into it. Pride came into it. And the thread that is developing in the psyche of the humans is getting stronger. *We speak from the*

Counsel.

The Counsel could understand, comprehend how "the devil" came to be called, because it was insidious and it seemed to be uncontrolled within the person. They seem to be victimized by it. And it was fascinating for the Counsel to watch this psychological shift in humans, and how they justified it or labeled it. It would be called evil; it would be called demon; it would be called devil; it would be called possessed. But these were all defences for behaviour that was indefensible, for behaviour that was so contravening of faith, and so contravening what generations had stood for.

It feels as if we are coming to a time where the tribe is quite distant from the original thought, the original equality, the original concept of the tribe. They heal from it, but it feels like they are quite close to being the furthest away from the ideal.

#7 Recording 41:30 *Death of Joseph of Egypt*

DS: And so we want to say that this one we speak of now, *we are not sure what his name was,* Joseph of Egypt?

He was of power, and he died in his wealthy place. He did not die a poor man. And there was great regret at his death. As if there was an experience, a vision, that let him see the errors, and the results of his errors; the selfishness, and the results of the selfishness. And we want to say, it carried to his soul, and gave his soul, *not his soul...* gave his consciousness, a fear of death. And that also feels new for those of faith, those of the tribe. It doesn't feel like it was normal to be afraid of their death, as if they knew it was a restoration.

But when this thread (*of power and selfishness*) came in, fear of death began to happen. And the soul, in an effort to ease this, created visions of death, to help the humans see. Sometimes it helped them to forgive before they died. But sometimes it did not. And it was a time when life and death and faith and God and evil became quite complicated. This is the best that we can explain.

As I witness the death of Joseph of Egypt, I am present and can sense how he was within his feelings, at his death moment. I can feel the presence of the fear of death and can also sense that this is out of the ordinary. I can sense the influence of the soul here, and that the soul is offering this vision of his life lived to Joseph as a means of making peace with himself at his death.

It feels to me that this fear of death is a result of Joseph realizing the influence of power, of selfishness and that Joseph is seeing these influences clearly. It seeds within Joseph of Egypt fear at his death. I can sense that the presence of the soul is to assist Joseph in his dealing with this fear of death. Again, fear of death feels unusual here.

As I perceive this vision, which is a life review, I can sense a realization that creates reaction within Joseph. In this case, the reaction is fear at the death moment.

It feels to me as if this is yet another moment of evolution within mankind. To have, at the death moment, a vision, a life review, which leads to realizations and understandings. I can sense an interaction between the soul of Joseph at his death and Joseph himself, and this feels new to me as if the presence of the soul has not been so involved before.

227

DR: Was Joseph of Egypt a Hebrew?

DS: He was. It feels like his faith was Hebrew. His integrity was of God. I am not sure he wore it like a badge of honour, but neither did he deny it. He was a quiet Hebrew. Because he more often did defend those of Hebrew and negotiate for those of Hebrew. But as he became seduced by the power, it was like the Hebrew became more quiet within him.

#7 Recording 45:40 *Two Josephs?*

DR: These two stories of Joseph, son of Jacob, and Joseph in Egypt in the Hebrew Bible, these were inflated and intermixed into one story, it seems like.

DS: We would say yes, for all we can see, the only similarity between the two is the dedication to the faith, and the closeness to God. Joseph, murdered by his brothers, wanted to be the hand of God. And the Joseph of Egypt wanted to do God's work. So, there are similarities here.

We are not sure if it was deliberate that one story was woven from the other. We're not sure. We don't see the connection. I can't see where one story became the other story. I can't see the one who wrote the story. I can't see the one who put the two together. I can't see that action.

When I ask questions, I don't get answers to them. I can't see a connection in the tribe, or a connection in the family. Were they trying to connect the tribe to this Joseph in Egypt, I do not, see? So I cannot give you an answer on that. I see there were two separate story lines.

DR: Was it around the same time period that these two things happened?

DS: Feels like the Joseph in Egypt was after the Joseph killed by his brothers, and not decades, perhaps five or ten years. No, not even ten, maybe five years. It was about the same time, which made them connectable.

We would say this to that. When we feel the depth of dedication and integrity in the Joseph killed by his brothers, this one could have become such a man (as Joseph of Egypt). His dedication to be the hand of God was that strong, and compassion was beginning to grow in his heart. Understanding was just seeded there. At the time of his death, he could have become such a man. So, we do not know if the story is a wish for what the man could have been, had he lived, or if it is another man entirely. We do not know.

But I can say, from being in the depth of the heart of Joseph killed by his brothers, that he could be such a man. He truly had that thread of the negative pride. He really had that well managed. The pride was always in the work and the work was through his hands, the hand of God. He didn't take it as a compliment to himself. There was always that distinction. And that bred within him a great strength that allowed him to manage that thread of negative energy, very, very adeptly. And in the beginning, the one in Egypt did as well, but he did succumb to it. This be the best that we can answer you.

DR: One final question about that. The one in Egypt, did he do dream interpretation?

DS: The first answer is no, but it feels like later he did. In the beginning, there was humble integrity, and he would not think to try. But as he became raised and saw the good work he was doing, and the people he had helped, the pride, that thread of self-pride got stronger, and he tried to help in other ways. But it doesn't feel like he did so in the beginning. It feels like he entered into other behaviours that were. *How do I explain this?* It feels like as he succumbed to the power, believed the power to be his, and he lost a little bit of that connection to it being God's work, God's hand. He started to then suppose what else he could be, what else he could do, how else he could help. Then he did enter into that realm of dreams and some healing. But at that point, it was more <u>his</u> interpretation than God's. He wasn't speaking for God at that point. It feels as if he had believed what was said about him and started to be a different man. But initially, no, he would not. He would not have even tried.

#8 Recording 5:05 *Origin of Joseph of Egypt*

DR: Can you explain the origin of this Joseph in Egypt?

DS: He feels to us to be raised Hebrew, but feels as if his father was Egyptian. He was not recognized by his father, and so stayed with his mother and her husband as family. There was, in his mother, a penance; a heart that felt penance was needed for her error, and treasured the gift of her son. And so, there was a demeanour about her of penance and appreciation. *His mother had found a peaceful way to live with her choices. And as part of her penance, she took upon herself to be sure her son was raised in the way of her faith.* She very much passed this on to her son. Her son was never overly robust, but she did teach him dedication, her ways, her beliefs. There was within him Egyptian blood that did not show itself till early adulthood. When we say show itself, we mean in his behaviour. There was a strength, a forthrightness, within him and there was some power. Not power in an egoic way, but a sense of strength within him and his character. And so, it was an interesting balance between the Egyptian blood and his mother's raising.

He was smart and caught onto things quickly. At some point he was made aware of his true parentage and his father, and that changed the course of his life. That occurred perhaps at sixteen years old. But it does not feel like the father acknowledged him that young. It feels more like it was a truthful revelation on his mother's part. And when that information became aware to him, it changed some of his focus and some of his ideas. *Change perhaps is not the right word.* It feels more like there were ideas within him that he was trying to grapple with, was conflicted with, and this helped him to understand, because there was some attraction to the Egyptian ways. There was some appreciation of the Egyptian ways. He then worked from the age of sixteen to early adulthood, to find a balance within himself, between these parts. There was always, always a holiness within him, but there was also a power within him, and it feels that is what made its way into the story of what you know as Joseph of Egypt.

DR: What was his mother's error?

DS: The error was the unfaithful act with the Egyptian man, unfaithful to her husband. She did reveal at the birth of the son the truth, because she was a truthful woman. And there was forgiveness in the family. We will not say one hundred percent, but there was acceptance and some forgiveness within the family. So, her error was her unfaithfulness.

DR: She and her husband were Hebrew, and the affair was

with an Egyptian?

DS: Yes, that is how we perceive it, that the fathering was Egyptian, and it brought to this one Joseph, the blending of the Egyptian blood with the Hebrew, the power with the godliness. It was an interesting blend in the energies.

DR: Did this Joseph rise to power in Egypt, to a powerful position?

DS: Yes, because once he understood who his father was, he then approached his father, and this created changes in his life. He was not recognized as the son of this Egyptian, but this Egyptian did bestow upon him an easier life. And what was interesting was that when the Egyptian bestowed upon him this life, he never lost that humble beginning. It gave him an opportunity to explore the power, the comfort of Egyptian life, but he managed to hold what his mother had taught him. And so, it was an interesting balance brought to this one.

DR: And so, this one married and he had sons?

DS: We are in agreement with that, yes.

DR: Do you have the name of the woman he married?

DS: *Uncertain.* Could be a name that started with J or S, but I am uncertain. I am not seeing a name.

DR: Did he have two sons named Ephraim and Manasseh?

DS: We want to say he had three sons, but it feels as if the first did not live much past childhood. *What were the other two names, please?*

DR: Ephraim and Manasseh.

DS: Manasseh feels correct. Ephraim is uncertain. There is a connection to him, but we cannot say yes to this being a son. It feels more like this was one under his tutelage or a ward. Not certain that this one was a son.

DR: Was his wife's name Asenath, with an' A', Asenath?

DS: It is odd. It feels like this is his wife, but this is not her birth name. Her birth name was much simpler. It feels like she was Hebrew, given an Egyptian name, as a disguise of sorts. And so, we want to say yes and no at the same time. This name is how his wife was introduced to all, but it is not the name he knew her by in his heart. It is not the name of her calling.

DR: What is the connection between Joseph in Egypt and the Hebrews who came down to live in Egypt, the sons of Jacob?

DS: Because of his mother, he favoured the Hebrews as he could, made for them a way, when he could. We do not see a direct connection, more a sense that he provided ease for them, contracts, work, solved problems, pointed them in the direction that would keep them out of the spotlight, protected them in a way.

He walked a fine line in his journey once he reached the important position. But still, even though there was a danger, *that might be too strong a word*, even though it could create conflict for him, he did still benefit, *there is the word I am looking for*, <u>benefit</u> these brothers. It was as if it was a test of his own character, put upon him by his own self, to prove to his mother he was still the son she raised. He was walking this line between what he believed and what the Egyptian life offered. And he tried to find a balance, and achieved it most of the time. There was a time where he did lose that balance. But for the most part, he did achieve it (the balance), until a certain age. And then there was a loss, and he succumbed to the seduction of the Egyptian ways and means.

DR: Jacob's sons, who then became the names of the heads of the twelve tribes, they came to Egypt separately, not by his invitation, but they came separately for other reasons?

DS: We do not see his invitation, no, but we do see that he was aware. As if he had a network of informers that kept him informed of what was occurring with the tribes. When he knew of their arrival, he did what he could to make it easeful for them. It was his way of paying tribute to his mother and her heritage.

DR: So that is when the Hebrews came to Egypt, and then they stayed there for hundreds of years, lived there in peace?

DS: Yes, he was one of four that were instrumental in maintaining a peacefulness about them, stopping or undoing rumors about them that would make them dangerous or coming to the spotlight. It feels like there were four different leaders that appreciated the truthfulness, the hard-working nature, the humbleness of the Hebrews. And so, they did have a good life there for a while.

DR: And these other leaders, they were in sequence, not in the same timeline. They were over different times?

DS: Yes, over different times. But there were influences. There was Joseph and there were two or three others that he knew, Egyptians, that he influenced. And so, there was always a spearhead of influence, but that had always two or three others of power, of voice, of reputation, that made it easeful for the Hebrews to be present there. There was appreciation for them, for their ways, for their truthfulness, for their hard work. They held their beliefs in demonstration and that was appreciated.

DR: So they lived a very simple life? They lived in buildings or stayed in their tents? What was their living arrangements and work?

DS: It feels as if the first generation were in the tents. The second generation came into small buildings, very small, humble. And then the third generation, it feels like there was a little bit larger space, but still very much humble, and they stayed in that. As if there was an allowance among the elders to move out of the tents and to start to enjoy presence in the city, but still on the edge of it, still not intertwined with the society completely. They did keep to themselves. They did participate, but did still keep to themselves in their privacy, in their private celebrations and in their private being of how they were true to their hearts.

DR: And this was basically the old ways which you mentioned before?

DS: Yes, and that is why the elders only let them go so far. They were offered bigger homes, larger buildings, but the elders would not. The elders allowed a certain level of protection, of home, of comfort, but no more. There was this maintenance of what was needed, not superfluous needs, what is needed. What is needed is allowed, but that which is beyond the need was not allowed. And so, there was a simplicity. And again, that was respected. It was consistent. It feels to us, for the most part, but we cannot say one hundred percent, everyone listened to the elders. And though there might have been one or two who moved off into the splendour of Egyptian life, for the most part, they did not. They maintained their way. They went into work; they were honest. They were honest labourers, and then they came home to their life, and they kept that separate. And the Egyptians appreciated that it was very quiet, a quiet and humble life. And they maintained that, as if those original beliefs the elders were holding on tight.

DR: What kinds of work did they do?

DS: There were stone masons. There was carpentry. There was animal husbandry. There weren't too many in servitude. It was more the kind of work they would have done in their own village. It was more manual labour. The elders wanted them to live a life where they earned their keep. It's not that the elders said no, but it was discouraged for someone to be a servant or to work in the splendour of Egypt. They were more in the maintenance, husbandry, carpentry, stone; more the labour jobs, because there was an honesty in it, there was a truthfulness in it, and there was a sense of having earned their keep.

When we explore the kind of work the Hebrews did in Egypt, I am present with them in their lives and can feel how important the need to "earn their keep" is. I can feel the elders truly determined to hold on to the old beliefs and the simplicity of life. And yet, I can also feel that there was not a "rule" as such about the work. It was more an encouragement, an appreciation for honest work. I do not perceive anyone being stopped from servant work, but it was not as appreciated, as respected, as manual labour. I can feel the simple value within them that simple labour brings. It feels as if it is an offering to God to be part of honest work, to be tending the animals or using carpentry to create something. I can feel how this keeps the old beliefs and simpler ways alive within them in Egypt.

DR: At this time period, did they have different tribes within the group?

DS: We would say yes to that because we are sensing four or five different elders, as if each elder had a family line or a tribe of family line that they were in charge of. There were four elders for certain, maybe three at times, maybe five at times. But it feels as if each elder was related to what you would call a tribe. It feels more like what we would call it a family.

Discussion

JOSEPH

#7 Recording 1:13:20 *Two Stories of Joseph*

DR: That was just crazy that they took two stories apparently and made it into one.

DS: Yes, and I couldn't find the connection between the two stories. It was like I was looking to see was it one of the brothers or was it someone of the same family trying to hide a shameful event? I couldn't see any link between the two stories.

DR: Right, and so in asking about these stories, I am trying to see if the stories happened; yes or no, or happened this way or that way, and in this case, it was two stories that were merged together.

DS: There definitely was someone in Egypt who did really good work for the Hebrews.

DR: Yes, but then in the Bible story, the brothers and Joseph reconciled, and they lived happily ever after, and they reunited with their father. So, everything was fantastic.

DS: Well, the first possibility is that I am just wrong, and I can fully accept that. But this felt so real to me, like it just felt that there was this thread of competition and the favouritism, and so much was being bestowed on Joseph and not on the brothers. It all felt very real to me.

#7 Recording 1:14:55 *Brothers Blinded by Fury*

DR: That's all in the stories, in the biblical stories.

DS: But the brothers didn't take him away to murder him. They took him away to teach him a lesson. It was really interesting to feel the blind fury. They literally were blinded to what they were doing. Their world literally went away from them. Their connection to conscience, to that part of the mind that says, "I have to be careful if I am going to do this", was gone. That connection to conscience had disappeared, and they were just blind to the moment. And it wasn't until he was struck and fell, and then they realized he was dead, that the blindness lifted. They couldn't leave him there. They wouldn't have left him there. They had to make up a story when they brought him back.

#7 Recording 1:15:45 *True Story Kept Hidden*

DR: The story in the Bible was that they threw him in a pit and some caravan came along, and they sold him into slavery, and he rose up.

DS: It felt like they considered leaving him, but that was because of the blindness. Once it had left them, they couldn't leave him. They couldn't do this to their brother. They couldn't just leave him. There was still enough integrity in each of the men. But it felt like it created a real breach in the family for, as we said, three generations.

DR: But according to what you were getting, the true story of the accidental death was never mentioned.

DS: No.

DR: It was hidden.

DS: Yes, it was hidden.

DR: It was hidden, and so when someone wrote the story they said, "Oh well, here is one story, here is another. Let's just put them together to make a good story."

DS: Again, if you think of the time, there was the birth of something they are calling "evil" that to the religious leaders, to the leaders of the tribe, they can't explain because it's never been within the tribe before.

So they were looking for ways to encourage people and to tell them stories that make them feel like they haven't lost their God, and they are not losing their way. It would make sense that two such stories would be put together, because this Joseph of the brothers was an incredibly controlled man and incredibly dedicated. And those same qualities were in the Joseph of Egypt. But what happened with the Joseph of Egypt is that the longer he was in Egypt, it was like he was infected, and started to believe in his own power. He started to believe that he was doing good, and it wasn't God's works. He lost his way.

#7 Recording 1:17:38 _Joseph Started to Mellow_

DR: For Joseph of the Bible, of the brothers, he was killed when he was an adult, like thirty years old?

DS: Yes, I would say this Joseph was a young adult. It didn't feel like he was yet married or had children, because that probably would have woken this Joseph out of strict faithfulness sooner. It felt like it was before that.

But it did feel like this Joseph was starting to feel compassion and starting to feel love which is why I asked if he was married, because I could feel love starting to blossom in him and compassion starting to blossom, which was softening his attitude of black and white. This softening was just seeded.

DR: A young man of twenty, twenty-five?

DS: Yes, I would say that. I would say whatever age that was when they started to look for a mate and started to see women and consider marriage. This Joseph was just at that point. And he was softening quite nicely and that would have allowed him to be a better husband than he would have been five years before, because then the black and white was really black and white.

This one, this Joseph, did not compromise. He didn't have compassion. For him there was one right way and he stuck by it. And his brothers and his father knew compromise. And he had disdain for his brothers for their compromise. This Joseph would never do that with this father, for he could accept his father. But with his brothers, there was some disdain and that was interpreted by the brothers to mean that he was better than them. Which wasn't what he was doing. He just didn't understand why they were not adhering to the law. The law is clear.

I mean if you think of a law that says you can't cut your hair, and you cut your hair, you've broken the law. There's no grey area there. Don't cut your hair. I am not saying that was one of the laws, but it was that clear to him. You did or you didn't.

And so, for this Joseph, to just start having the seeds of compassion and love beginning, this was going to change him as a man, and it was just all starting. If his brothers could have seen inside his heart, they would have seen he did not mean anything that they interpreted. And he just surrendered to the actions of his brothers.

#8 Recording 1:12:20 *Error in the History of the Bible*

DR: That whole Joseph story was absolutely fascinating because the twelve tribes came from Jacobs' sons, Joseph and the rest of the sons. But two of the twelve tribes were headed by Ephraim and Manasseh, but they were actually, in the Bible, Joseph's sons, grandsons of Jacob. They became two of the twelve heads of tribes of Israel. So, Jacob <u>grandfathered</u> them in; Jacob said, "I consider them my sons so now they can be equal with my sons." But they weren't his grandsons, they were the other Joseph's sons.

DS: The one was a son, but the other one, he was more like a ward.

DR: But you see how they intertwined stories, and they made Joseph of Egypt sons to be...

DS: And that could have ever been from someone who said, "Well Jacob would never have made them leaders of the tribe. They had to be Joseph's sons, and so this has to be wrong." They must be, and then the story changed. I can see that sometimes the stories are told to make fit what they want to purport.

DR: Exactly.

DS: There is no maliciousness in it though. At least none that I could feel.

DR: No, but these were the only two that were grandsons, not sons. The Bible kind of twisted it around and made it work.

Section Six

MOSES – NO TEN PLAGUES

The story of Moses begins in Egypt at a time when the Pharaoh ordered all male Hebrew babies to be thrown into the Nile.

A man of the house of Levi went and married a Levite woman. The woman conceived and bore a son; and when she saw how beautiful he was, she hid him for three months. When she could hide him no longer, she got a wicker basket for him and caulked it with bitumen and pitch. She placed the child in it and placed it among the reeds by the bank of the Nile. And his sister stationed herself at a distance to learn what would befall him. (Exodus 2:1-4)

DR: And so, begins the incredible story of Moses and the exodus of the Hebrews from the land of Egypt. This is the seminal or central story of the Jewish people. It is the second beginning after the start of the religion under Abraham, and the beginning of the laws, the moral codes, now starting to be written.

The story contains many events and miracles that are hard to accept today. The first question is why would the Pharaoh's daughter raise an orphaned boy, knowing it was Hebrew and that her father decreed all Hebrew babies to be killed? The miracles include the plagues visited upon the Egyptians by God, the display of sorcery (turning staffs into snakes), and the parting of the Red Sea, allowing the Hebrews to escape in the nick of time.

In asking about the Moses story, I was particularly interested in the events described of the Pharaoh's daughter rescuing a Hebrew infant, the plagues visited by God, and the parting of the Red Sea, if they happened as written, or if there was a more plausible explanation for these happenings. Did Moses and the escaped tribes really wander in the desert for forty years? If so, how did they get enough food and water for such a journey that lasted more than one generation?

#5 Recording 3:44 *Story of Moses*

DR: I want to explore the whole story of Moses and the biblical exodus starting with if you could explain the origin, the birth of Moses.

DS: Moses was born at a time in your world where discoveries and explorations were expanding. Moses was born to a family of the old ways and the Old Faith and there were conflicts around his family, where the explorations of possibility were beginning to conflict with the Old Faiths.

Moses was raised by the Old Faith. Moses was influenced by the new explorations and new possibilities in his young adult life. There were conflicts and contests, and there were challenges to the gods, as if in the expanding time, challenges were being put upon the gods to prove themselves.

Those of the Old Faith, the ways of Eden, stayed away from such contests. But the young adults were exploring, and Moses was among the explorers. But as the explorations and contests continued, the challenges were not always met by the gods. And so, those with stronger minds created new ideas, new beliefs. The time of Moses' upbringing was conflicting and challenging. There was chaos at the edges and that chaos continued to grow.

In the early years of his manhood, thirty something, Moses was touched by the Old Faith again. He found the challenges in the new ways were touched by the chaos, and he found it wanting, and returned to the Old Faith. There was a strength in his manhood that grew from this return. The chaos also led to challenges in the tribes, and then those that ruled the tribes. And chaos started to grow. Those that were of the Old Faith moved as far away as they could, but the chaos still touched many. Pilgrimages were the way those of the Old Faith escaped for short periods of time, and then returned.

The story of Moses, at this point, is where it began. He is

portrayed as a singular voice in the tribe. Our (the Counsel's) witnessing of this did not see such. He was a strong man of faith, but he also challenged the gods for provings.

I can feel the growth that is causing people to question, what is called "challenge the gods". It is fascinating to see that blind faith acceptance is weakening and new ideas are being born. I can feel a growth energy. I can feel a power beginning to grow in each person that seems to fuel their "challenge to the gods". Fascinating to witness growth in this way.

The mind of humans was developing quickly and the relationship with the gods through the nature was being lost. For the intelligence was finding ways to have water in the dry spells, so that they did not wait for the god of rain. Inventions were coming now. Necessity called those inventions into creation. And the evolution of the mind of man was fascinating to watch in its speed. How quick they learned. But as the mind learned, the faith was jeopardized. We will not say faith was lost to the tribe, but it was jeopardized, and there were fewer and fewer of the Old Faith.

It feels to me to truly be a time of evolution in mankind.

In a retreat, Moses did seek to reconnect to the Old Faith, to those he had heard stories about from Eden. And visions, **memories** opened to him. He, in the stories that were told, called them visions. They were <u>memories</u> from within his own cellular structure – memories of what had been in Eden, in relation to the Earth herself. His memories opened, and his mind was flooded with realizations and understandings. This was his miracle: comprehension, understanding, wisdom. He <u>remembered</u> the old ways with strength. He <u>remembered</u>

Eden. He <u>remembered</u> Adam. He <u>remembered</u> the way. It took him weeks to synthesize. But as we have said, the brains were so active.

He shared these visions with two others. We will call them memories, for that's what they were. He shared his memories with two others, male. And in the conversations, they tried to make sense of what the memories meant. He shared the memories with his mother. This was the only woman he shared them with. And, as the memories were discussed, ideas of how to strengthen the Old Faith for the new generation were discussed. Rules did come, but not in the form that the story portrays.

Rules came from the memories, from understanding the memories, in trying to make them applicable now. As we have said to you before, as the brains grew, simple living was lost, and so the simple way of living was lost. The memories showed Moses the way of living in its simplicity and the rules were the result of three minds, one of which was Moses', trying to re-institute the different behaviour based upon the old ways.

Later generations, in an effort to make the rules compulsory, to add more power to the rules, to reassert the power of gods, created the story you know of tablets, and that the rules were written in stone, to make them more abiding; to make them more commandments, to take away the choice. For by this stage of journey, Moses, in his latter stages of manhood and further, choice seemed to be becoming an evil, for the brains were developing so quickly. Inventions were coming. There were so many choices.

Power was starting to be explored. And the commandments,

the laws written from memory, were basic, practical ways to live with integrity and respect. They were adapted to exert more influence and later control. But at the heart of their creation, it was a good intention, restoring a pillar of respect and living in the old way of Eden.

But the story of Moses came out of his re-connection to memories, his memories, the memories passed down. They were called visions because memories would not have been understood. And as Moses perceived them, they were like visions. Visions of other times, visions of other worlds, faces to those that had only been names. And so, vision was an adequate word, but the influence was increased, the control, the command of it was increased.

In the next breath the Counsel returns my focus to Moses himself and his personal story. I am with him as he retreats and begins to seek for more peace from the chaos. I am present to the opening of his memories and can see them flow to him like visions.

Then everything slows down again, and I am present to Moses after his visions/memories and can feel him sorting through this in his mind. It is most interesting that this time of great growth of mind also served Moses, himself. For it enables his mind to synthesize through all these visons/memories and come to an understanding of them.

In the thoughts of Moses, he seems to boil it down to the need for all to be simple again. I can also see the two men with Moses and witness the sharing, the discussion, and the ideas that flow. Again, this is all coming from the same "growing mind" but with these men, including Moses, the growing mind is being focused differently, and so the old ways are being seen in a different way. I *can feel that the three of them together are able to witness the chaos that is beginning to grow and together they arrive at the idea of rules to install the simplicity again. **I do perceive that these "rules" become what are called the commandments in the original myth.***

I can feel their passionate agreement that simplicity is the answer and that the rules/laws they create are seeking to make compulsory the simple ideas of respect for one another and simpler living. It is fascinating to watch this growth of understanding within the three of them. Again, I perceive it in a fast forward way, so I do not mean to imply that all was achieved in one meeting. It was not.

I can feel a momentum that started at the time and then carried mankind into these new directions. There is a sense of momentum (movement) that then simply carries mankind with it, into power, into choice, into invention, and I can even sense it carrying mankind into this modern world.

#5 Recording 17:27 *Parting of the Red Sea*

DS: The miracle of the parting of the sea was a weather phenomenon, and we (the Counsel) increased the impact of that weather phenomenon. The sea did not part, but flowed in various ways and revealed its base.

We do not revoke "miracle" in our words to you this day. We have not words to speak of miracles. We are observers through science, observers of phenomenon, evolution. We have observed the unexplainable, but over a course of study have most often been able to find explanation.

The Counsel has never spoken of their interference before now. In fact, they have been most adamant that they did not interfere in our evolution. But in these two paragraphs, I am fully in union with the Counsel and their words and attitude here are very different in feel to the rest of the information.

I could almost feel a slight resistance, a hesitation in their admitting interference. And then, their realization that this admittance could discount miracle. I can feel the strength and honesty of them then deliberately speak of themselves as scientists, so as not to discount the presence of miracles in our world, but to explain that miracles are not present in their world.

DR: The parting of the Red Sea, the movement of the waters enabled the Hebrews to escape across?

DS: These were those of the Old Faith, banding together to truly leave the new ways behind. For individually, Moses' family and others, tried to draw within themselves to their own family, but the influence of the chaos was too strong. And so, the movement enabled a tribe of the old ways to band together. And because of the force of what they called the Commandments, there was a select few that followed this path. More elders than youngers, but there were younger generations, and it was an amazing phenomenon to witness how the timing occurred and enabled them to reach a place so quickly and so freely.

Those of the new order were threatened by the old ways, once the families of the old ways banded together. We have no responses to the "miracle" of when the seas became calm again, the timing of it. But we cannot sanction the word miracle, we merely have not discovered the source of it.

As the Counsel shares their witness of this event (the parting of the sea), they are at odds to explain the timing of the return of the sea waters and how that occurred in such perfect time. It does feel like the Counsel cannot call it a miracle, but also cannot discount a miracle. It feels as if it leaves them with a scientific question. It is simply another puzzle for them to solve. It seems that mankind is a puzzle to the Counsel as we grow and change.

#5 Recording 21:50 *Moses Raised by Mother*

DR: So Moses was born an Egyptian, to Egyptian parents?

DS: We will say yes to this, but the mother was of the old ways. And so, we want to say, the mother was Egyptian, but not Egyptian. As if the mother was portrayed as such, but was not. She maintained something and schooled her son in this way.

Moses did not take to the schooling until the early stages of his manhood when he started to see the consequences of the chaotic choices. That is why when he prayed in his retreat and the memories were opened, he told his mother. She was able to confirm some of what he had seen. And that it was with the other two men that this became the laws.

The connection, the closeness between Moses and his mother is very obvious to me. I can feel their emotional bond and the trust he has of her. Even when Moses was rebellious or resistant to what she was teaching him, his trust and respect for her was so very strong, undeniable. It is the respect that is the most tangible. I can feel the depth of the respect. It feels like another kind of love.

DR: Can you name or describe the other two men who he revealed his visions to?

DS: One has the feeling of a rabbi or priest, a holy man. This one was a little older than Moses and knew more of the stories. His memories were not awakened, but he remembered more of the stories.

The other has the feeling of brother, brethren, not sure if this one is brother by blood. This one is slightly younger than Moses. It feels as if in the three of them, there are three generations. The elder has the passed down story memories, conscious memories. With Moses, unconscious memories have opened. And the younger believes and is willing, would love for his memories, visions, to open as Moses' did. There is enthusiasm in the younger man, a bit of idealism.

In Moses there is strength and determination, deep faith and belief that change is needed. And the elder is like confirmation. This one remembers stories and names and has made a point of keeping these alive in his memory.

As we describe the two men who Moses revealed his visions to, I can feel, literally feel how they each complete or add to each other. As if in each man, a piece of the puzzle is contained. In the elder, the conscious memories as they were passed down that then feeds to Moses, more clarity for his visions. And then the younger man seems to represent where this is all going to go. The three of them form a circle of sacred understanding that so naturally leads them to action, to the commandments. The connections between the three of them are so obvious to me. Fascinating.

It is this circle of three that leads the tribe to their next chapter of existence. And in a human way, the support they offer each other nourishes each of them to move forward and strengthens within each man their bravery and confidence in their decisions. It is as if the three of them create together, one leader, and such a strong leader. The tribe(s) benefited from this strength.

#5 Recording 25:30 *Moses' Companions*

DR: Is either of these Aaron or Joshua?

DS: *Show me the elder, please.* Aaron. Joshua. Possibly Aaron, but I am not sure. If not Aaron, then of the bloodline of Aaron.

DR: The story of Moses being born to a Hebrew woman and placed in a basket in the water is just a myth?

DS: He is born to a Hebrew woman, but the basket is the myth.

#5 Recording 26:27 *Evolution/The New Faith*

DR: The old faith came from Eden on down through Abraham who awakened his memories all the way down to Moses, who remembered through his visions.

DS: Yes.

DR: What was the new way of thinking, the new faith that was so troubling?

DS: Choice. Invention. Selfishness. Individual choice. The beginnings of the loss of cohesiveness in the tribe, cohesiveness of the village. Threads of inequality, some more favoured, some less favoured, the beginnings of this.

It occurred innocently through invention, through inspired inventions. And then those who were inspired to invent became better than others who did not, became more important. And with the importance came influence, wealth, power. And choice seemed to breed selfishness, ownership.

With the old ways, there was no owner of anything. All worked together as one. We will not say that individual families did not have their heirlooms, their woven blankets, and their clay pots from generations before that belonged to their family. But such ownership did not create inequality. The birth of invention was the seed of inequality, and this was the chaos that invaded.

DR: By inventions you mean physical implements that made life better, easier for farming, building, whatever?

DS: Yes. And artistry, embellishment, ideas of how to use things, different minerals, different ways. Curiosity and invention, it began so innocently.

But again, as we have spoken before, there is a presence of an evolutionary energy in the Earth. And so everything that is discovered evolves. And so that which started innocently, out of curiosity and need, EVOLVED into more and more of what it could become. And inequality was born.

And then inequality evolved. As we witnessed this place called Earth, it is quite fascinating to see how every attitude, learning, behaviour, invention, creation, EVOLVES. The aliveness of your planet is remarkable.

In this discussion about what was causing the chaos, about what the new faith was, the Counsel is very clear. I am witnessing the birth of change through invention. In an overview, I am seeing creativity start, inspired creativity, and from that inventions arrive. Life is improved but what is fascinating to me is to see how this creative innovation creates inequality. How those that are inspired to invent become better than those that do not. So, it is not the inventions that cause the chaos, but the reactions to those inventions. The judgments that are made concerning these inventions, this creativity. The birth of inequality, I can see it, feel it and it grows fast!

As with the Counsel, I can feel the effect of EVOLUTION on all things of the Earth. It is truly a force on the Earth, and I can feel it as a force. It cannot be stopped, and neither would anyone think to stop it, for it is as much a part of the Earth as flowers blooming in the spring. It is something of the Earth that makes the Earth so unique.

And in the EVOLUTION of mankind, our minds, our creativity is born. It is another place for EVOLUTION to expand and grow itself. The synchronicity of the growth of mankind, our minds, our creativity, and the growth of EVOLUTION itself is truly amazing!

I can only find a natural movement of EVOLUTION. I sense no outside influence, be it the Counsel or CREATION itself. EVOLUTION is just as it is and all it can do is take something and urge it to evolve, to grow, to become more. I have never witnessed anything like EVOLUTION before. It is alive. It is a natural urge on the Earth for all those of the Earth.

#5 Recording 30:52 *Egyptian Mystery Schools*

DR: Did Moses learn the secrets of the Egyptian mystery schools? The Egyptians had mystery schools where their priests were trained in deep secrets. Did Moses participate, learn some of these secrets?

DS: He did, not from the schools themselves, but from one who attended the schools. The younger man of the three had some experience with the mysteries. And it feels as if Moses' visions and the younger man's beginnings of understanding of the mysteries came together.

We witnessed the mystery schools as the birth of science. Each mystery, from where we observed it, was explainable. They were not aware of what they were handling for they knew not what energy was. But it was science that the mysteries were exploring. Because it was unknown, because energy was not a word or concept at the time, it became a mystery. But they were learning to direct energy. They were learning the aliveness of all things. And these were the beginnings of the mystery.

There is pleasure and approval from the Counsel that EVOLUTION is now taking the tribes into this exploration. Interesting that I do not feel this as a judgement of Earth or of mankind, but a pleasure to watch EVOLUTION now move in this direction. Fascinating because I can feel the depth of the science and need for explanations that is contained in the Counsel. I cannot feel any understandings of magic, miracles, or mystery within the Counsel. For them, everything can be explained, eventually.

#5 Recording 32:53 *Enslavement from Inequality*

DR: The whole mythology of the Hebrews, part of them moving to Egypt and then later becoming enslaved, can you explain that?

DS: Enslavement came from inequality. Those who were not inspired to invention were deemed less worthy. And so those who were not part of the wealth that invention birthed, served the inventors. They were treated as ignorant. And many of those labeled ignorant were of the old ways, the Old Faith. For the Old Faith was about the living of life, compassion, kindness, respect. There was no excess in the Old Faith. And so those who lived to the Old Faith served those who lived to the new inventions and wealth, and the inequality evolved.

What made them perceived as slaves was their adherence to the old ways, was their loyalty to one another, was their loyalty to compassion, to kindness and to respect. The inequality did not grow among them, for all that was received was always shared.

As Moses came to his awakening of memory, he shared it. He was careful who he shared it with, but he shared it, nonetheless. He did not make himself king. There was not inequality in the Hebrews. They were simple-minded, but they were not stupid. They were not unintelligent. They lived with more simplicity and so they became without, because of how the society started to evolve. And so, they were servants, and they were in service to those of the wealth.

DR: Were the old ways and the Egyptian beliefs before this new way took effect because the inventions? Were they compatible? The old ways that Moses remembered and the Egyptian old gods and beliefs, were they the same or compatible?

DS: No. The old ways challenged the new ways. Their adherence to the simplicity of life was seen as a judgment of those who lived a life of more, of invention, of sparkle, of artistry, of gold.

But as the memory has shown, those of the Old Faith just lived in a simple way. They did not use decoration, but this did not speak that decoration was wrong. It was not their way. But the difference was antagonizing. And it was interpreted by those who left the old ways for the new ways, that those who were not wearing a band of gold, or changing their clothing, or using the inventions, that they were critical of those that did. It is not our sense they were. It was more that they simply wanted to be left to live their way, but they were perceived as a threat to their judgment.

The old ways' memories at the time were contained within the cellular memory of all. Moses was not special. Moses sought to understand. And that need to understand gave him a command for the memories to open. These people of the old ways, living the old way, became like an unconscious thorn in the deepest memories of the new ones. And they felt threatened by that because they represented something that those of the new ways wanted to simply forget and move on from, evolve away from, believing the inventions and the inequality was meant to be. It was the EVOLUTION. It was how it was to change. And those that wanted to stay out of it were perceived as a threat, because they inadvertently and unconsciously were disturbing the memories in every single person.

DR: But before this change took place in Egyptian society, morality, was the older Egyptian ways like the old faith, similar to what the Hebrews had?

DS: Yes, there is a branch of the Hebrew family, when Eden ended, and the pairs went different ways. There is a connection to what you are calling Hebrews and what you are calling Egyptians. There's a connection there, way back in its beginning. And that kept the memories of Eden alive, so that through the generations of the Egyptians, the original memories were seeded in the cellular memory.

Every human has the original memories. They choose to ignore them, to keep them dormant. The presence of the Hebrews threatened the dormancy of the memories. It created a discomfort in those of the new ways. The discomfort we are suggesting, comes from the unconscious disturbance of the original memory, disturbing its slumber. And so they needed to remove the threat that brought the discomfort.

And all that the Hebrews, as you are calling them, wanted was to live the way they lived. We will not say there was no judgment among the Hebrews, but there was not the judgement that is portrayed. They just wanted to be left to their ways. They wanted to leave them (the Egyptians) to their ways.

There were those who saw the ways of affluence as negative because of the chaos it brought, because of the inequality it bred; because of the disregard it bred, and so they wanted to be nothing but away from it. And yet the Hebrews were determined to be a threat, and so they were wanting to be, not extinguished, but there was a school of thought that those who would not leave the old ways should leave the world. And there were those in the Egyptian ways who saw this as their duty. And so part of the escape was lifesaving for the Hebrews, to prevent an extinction.

I find it interesting that the Counsel does not answer the question of the Old Faith of Egypt in a clear fashion. They keep our focus on what they feel is most important. And in this case, it is a quick overview of how EVOLUTION was involved.

I can feel how strong EVOLUTION is as it continues to lead mankind and their story. I can feel the impetus, the nudging, the push to evolve. As if there is little choice but to feel what they are feeling. I can actually feel the resistance to that movement that is held by those of the old ways. It is as if their faith strengthens them to resist the movement of EVOLUTION itself.

As the Counsel speaks of the "original memories seeded in our cells", I can feel the truth of them. I can feel the depth of these memories and how they are anchored within those of Eden. As I continue to follow the Counsel in its words, I can feel a link that these memories create. It feels as if the memories link everyone, as if they are in fact "shared" memories. I "see" that those memories are a presence in the core of each person who originated in Eden.

The Counsel watches and waits. I can feel their interest, even their fascination of this stage of our evolution. I can also feel that they are, once again, witnesses only, with no interference.

But it all comes because throughout all time in your world, there have been those who will always hold the memories closer to the surface. Who will always remember the truth of life. And they are always deemed a "threat" because they disturb the dormant original truth of life.

The truth, the original truth of life has evolved. We have watched it. It is magnificent. But there has also evolved an attachment to the new way of being, an inequality to the new way of being that it is <u>better.</u> That there is something less than, in the origins. Which is not the truth. And so the defense of the new way, the defense of the inequality, defense of the right to richness, of the right to inequality. The defense of it has always been, defense "against" the original idea of life. **And**

each time <u>the</u> Jesus, <u>the</u> Mohammed, <u>the</u> Buddha, each time memories have surfaced in a person; they are revered because they remember what others know is there but can't find. <u>Or they are a threat for those who do not want to remember and want only what is now.</u>

And so in the evolution of your planetary space, in the evolution of your civilization, there will always be beings who remember the original idea of life. It is part of the evolution, the change and then the reinstatement of the origins of life. So that the evolved, invented new life can also contain the compassion and respect of the origins of life.

We have not understood and still do not understand … It is why we are so intent upon connections to the humans as we are talking to you. <u>We do not understand how EVOLUTION still requires the origins of life to be kept alive.</u> It isn't an evolution away from something. **It's an evolution to a growth of something, that the original thought of life wants to be maintained within the center of it.**

But it just seems as if, as the evolution of your planetary space, of your civilization, of invention, of curiosity, of artisan, as that has evolved, somehow it is threatened by the origin of life. And that evolution itself is an interesting conflict that we monitor.

Those who have come to the original memories of life have been put into monasteries, have been put into the nunneries, have been put into the religions, have been put into these sacred spaces, but they have always been kept away from the life that has evolved. **And so, those of wealth are not the shaman. Those of wealth are not the ones who know of the origins of life.** It is a fascinating quandary of your planet.

The entire concept of EVOLUTION is at the root of what the Counsel wants to understand. I can feel this to be true. It is the EVOLUTION on the Earth that draws them to us. It is how the EVOLUTION interacted with the Counsel's original experiment that keeps the Counsel present with us.

The Counsel allows me to be within them as they demonstrate and explain what they believe. That belief is that as the new ways evolve, there is meant to be a core of the old ways contained within it all. As this belief is revealed, I can feel the truth of it. Truth, in this instance, feels clear, concise, and leading. I can almost feel the depth of the Counsel's witnessing that has led them to this belief. I can feel the weight of our entire history sitting within this belief. I am almost overcome by the weight of it. <u>This idea of the old ways and the new ways partnering is from the Counsel and what they have come to understand.</u>

DR: There was a group of Hebrews or tribe that moved from Canaan to Egypt, and they were compatible with the Egyptian society and then things changed during their sojourn there?

DS: Yes, exactly. There was this inventive artisan evolution in the Egyptians, and those of the Hebrews did not participate, because they watched its influence with their youngsters and kept them away from it. They watched selfishness. They watched inequality. They watched disrespect. They watched one choice overrule another choice. And so, they became leery of choice, independence, separation. And they wanted to move to a place where they could be as they once were. And we are certain that it has not been lost on anyone on your planet that the Hebrews, and the land of the Hebrews, is land of the "what is real". It is called Is-rael, but it is what is real. Because what is real was the origins of life.

And so, through crossing the sea, the Hebrews went to a place where that which was of Egypt would not follow. The gold would not be brought, because the Hebrews did not hold the gold. They did not have the wealth; they did not have the invention. They held to the old ways.

The Hebrews were perceived as a threat and that is why there was the war. That is why there was, for some, a decision made that they must be made extinct. They were perceived as a threat. Just as the teachings of Jesus were perceived as a threat. Just as the teachings of Buddha were done in some isolated place. Always when the origins of life memories surface, it has a mechanism to isolate. We have not and cannot explain it to you. But we have witnessed it over and over and over again as we have studied your place.

The Counsel explains how the changes in Egypt led to the Hebrews leaving Egypt. As the Counsel speaks about the results connected to the origins of life memories, I can sense within the Counsel a bit of frustration, and the sensation of being perplexed. They truly were witness to something they did not understand. And the Counsel in a place of not understanding is not a comfortable place for them.

I am left with a sense that we truly were, from the Counsel's perspective, within an experiment which they did not know how it would unfold. But simultaneously, I can sense that there is a supportive wonder coming from another level of energy that I can only call CREATION itself. I am left with a sense of what I can only call the miraculous, as I witness the growth of mankind from Eden to now. And then such a sensation of not being alone in our evolution, although I could not name what keeps us from being alone. It is simply a sensation that we are not alone in any of this evolution. I feel comforted by that feeling.

DR: How large was the group who left Egypt and were they pursued by the Egyptians?

DS: There was pursuance. It was a group of Egyptian warriors who believed the threat (of the Hebrews) so strong, that there was an extinction order given. Almost a similar thing to your history when the Christians moved to the Arabian states.

As the Counsel explains the pursuit of the Hebrews, I can see the similarity to another time in history. My words are literal in that I can see the knights on horses. I can see the killing. I can see the savagery. The Counsel does not refer to one specific time in history but a similar time, the word I am searching for is allowed to surface – the Crusades.

The hatred, the threat, the chasing, and the killing is not similar to any one event in our history but to many events. And these types of events the Counsel has witnessed often in our history and yet, still, I do not feel judgment from the Counsel.

They followed the Hebrews and wanted to kill as many as they could to prevent them from rooting someplace else. They were perceived as a threat. There was a clan within the Egyptians or a part of the tribe, who were believers of this. These believers saw the Hebrews as much more of a threat than the general Egyptians would. And they were the ones that took an army and chased them. They were the ones that began the wars that followed for so many generations.

And the timing of the sea we cannot explain. A miracle perhaps, but we do not have that belief so we cannot call it such. But they found their place. And there was ...*show me the clan lines, please. Show me the families and the tribes...*

The sense I'm getting is that there were eleven different family lines within the Hebrews that crossed the Sea. There was the presence of eleven different family lines. I cannot tell you how many people, but there were the seeds of eleven different families.

DR: Did these become the twelve tribes?

DS: Yes, these became the twelve tribes. There were eleven besides Moses, so Moses was the twelfth.

DR: Were there Hebrews who remained in Canaan, in Israel throughout this whole time when part of the group was in Egypt?

DS: Yes, there were Hebrews who stayed. Though they knew inequality, they lived a good life, and simply believed that they were living a good life which is what their God wanted. And so, they continued in their simplicity, in their service.

There were also those who strove to become what Egyptians were, and so they stayed as they saw that was their only avenue to leave what they were and become something else. There were those who were afraid, who knew of the extinction order, and so were simply afraid and stayed under the protection of their Egyptian lords.

DR: But were there some Hebrews who never left Canaan, and were rejoined when the ones who escaped Egypt went back to Canaan? Were there some who maintained their beliefs and never left Canaan or Israel?

DS: *Show me what he is speaking about, please?* Can you ask that another way?

DR: When Hebrews originally went down to Egypt to live there, were there some Hebrews who did not go with them to Egypt originally?

DS: Yes. Three family lines? Maybe five. A small number who were content with what was. Yes, yes there were.

DR: Did they maintain themselves? Did they rejoin Moses and his group when Moses came back through?

DS: They heard the stories of Moses and there was reverence, because the stories they heard were not the truth; they were made more of. There were some who joined Moses. And there were some who believed the over-telling of the story and so stayed even more simple. We would say perhaps two-thirds joined Moses, and one-third did not.

#5 Recording 54:42 *Ten Plagues*

DR: Can you explain the myth of the ten plagues that were put upon the Egyptians?

DS: There is such sadness upon hearing this question.

Those who needed the old ways to be wrong, those who needed the new ways to be right, those who needed the Hebrews to be a threat, created stories that made them a threat. They created stories that made them (the Hebrews) dangerous and deserving of extinction. There were, in the inequality beliefs, ideas that those who lived a simple life carried disease, and so they simply built upon that idea. These are myths, blamed upon the Hebrews, to make the Hebrews even more dangerous, even more of a threat. **The threat of the Hebrews was their simplicity in their faith, nothing more.**

As this question is answered my focus is turned again upon the Hebrews, not the Egyptians. I can feel that my focus is put upon the Hebrews because this part of the story is to slight the Hebrews even further. To lay blame on the Hebrews and nourish more hatred towards them. And so my sense is that the victim in this story is not the Egyptians, but the Hebrews. It feels to me as if the Egyptians are the creators of the story. I cannot sense any participation of a god, or CREATION, or anything else. It feels to be manmade, a made-up story to slight the Hebrews and make them even more threatening to Egypt.

DR: How long did Moses and his tribes journey through the desert back to Canaan/Israel?

DS: One full generation, into the second generation. So those that were children with Moses, were beginning to know their grandchildren when they arrived. It wasn't a journey. It was a movement, a settling, a movement, a settling, a movement, a settling. It wasn't day after day of journey. It wasn't a trip. It was movement, settling, and then movement, further settling.

Something else was directing Moses at this point. Originally, it was the memories of the origins of life, of Eden's memory. But through his travels, once his memories were freed, it was about the simplicity of life. And Moses was now seeking a place that would support life as they wanted it. And so twice they stopped at a place they felt would serve, but as the seasons moved, they realized it would not, and movement was needed again.

There were two settlings before they arrived at what you are calling Canaan or Israel. There were two settlements before that. There was one full generation and the beginning of the next generation before they arrived at the place that was truly able to sustain the simplicity and the richness of life that they wanted. And so, they were traveling, geographically exploring. And the first settling came when they thought this land would support them. And then with the seasonal change, realized it wouldn't. Then the entire village of them moved again, much larger now. And then they found another place to settle, did not stay long, and then moved finally.

DR: Are these two places known... where they stopped and tried to settle?

DS: One feels like a desert, nomadic, with small portions of water. *Is there a place here now that you could show me?* No, this place feels like a desert; it feels undeveloped.

The second place had more promise and very few stayed. It feels as if it had water, and so lushness. But the waters dried. Something changed in the climate and the waters were lost. And those that didn't follow Moses to the final place, became nomadic. So again, it feels like a desert to me. It doesn't feel developed.

I witness their settling and then moving again. I can feel the tribe's faith in Moses and so the first move is without resistance. But the second move, there is more hesitation. They were more settled and to move again was difficult. And then the third move, I can actually feel the resistance to moving again, and I can see some do not join them. Some move away on their own and I can feel the weakening of their faith, not in their God, but in Moses, the man. It has been too long for some of them now to still trust Moses as they once did.

I can see them move off on their own and become nomadic and in this nomadic existence, they are under their own choice, their own power. I can feel their "choice" strengthen and they are less followers now and more choosing their own path. I can feel EVOLUTION at work once again.

DR: So how did they feed themselves throughout this whole journey?

DS: There were groups of men that went out seeking water, fish, habitat, growth, green. And so there was a sense of barter, weavings that were traded for food. There were interactions with nomads. There were interactions with merchants crossing the desert. And some of the handcrafts were traded for food. And then there were these groups that went out in search of animals, of water, of fish. They had almost a nomadic way of self-care.

DR: In the Bible when Moses speaks to God, God speaks to Moses. Can you explain this phenomenon?

DS: When one allows the origins of life memories, one then has an ability to communicate with so many. With Moses, his faith in the origins and the old ways bonded him to a being he knew to be God. It was a benevolent being, who used his wisdom and his experience to guide Moses and his tribe. The perception of this one as a god is understood, but really it was a being of wisdom that understood CREATION. And to understand CREATION, one can command creation. And so this one, in benevolence to Moses and his journey, took to serve Moses by commanding creation, thereby becoming god.

But as we have said before, every human contains the memories of the origins of life. And once the origins of life memories are accessed, CREATION becomes accessible, and co-creating becomes possible.

The being that Moses came to call God, was not the Counsel.

DR: Moses felt he was speaking to God, then. That's fantastic.

#9 Recording 1:02:52 *Origin of The Laws*

DR: Can you comment on the laws, like the kosher laws, circumcision, all the rules in the book of Leviticus? What was the origin of those?

DS: *The book of Leviticus, please.*

These were an attempt to find cause for the loss of the gifts of Eden. These were an attempt to recover. The laws you speak of, the kosher laws, all of these laws, there was an awareness in the elders that something was being lost of the simplicity, or the strength. By this point when Leviticus was created, the gifts of Eden were well-fading, evolved, almost to the point of only being a memory or a story. And within the thinking mind, there was analysis and judgment, trying to find a way to restore what was lost. And in trying to find a way to restore, blame was laid, looking for a cause that would have created the loss, and then how to undo that. So, the laws were created trying to purify, trying to clarify, trying to restore the pure simple purification that was at the beginning.

There was not an understanding at this stage of the consciousness that Adam and Eve brought. It had been taken over by EVOLUTION by this point and the mind had its shadow places, and judgment was stronger. Through judgment, blame was stronger, and through blame the laws were created, seeking to purify, hoping it would restore what was lost. The blaming and judging were incorrect and so the laws did not do what they hoped they would do.

To this day, there is still a desire for purity, and it is not only in your tribes of Hebrew. It is in other tribes of your planet who seek to find something that was lost. But it has become warped and twisted. As we witness it from the Counsel, there is this deep-seeded awareness of great gifts having been lost, but no memory of what they are. And the judging mind simply blames and believes purification will restore them. And so, purification is tried over and over again in your world, because there is this innate sense within yourselves of a memory of something that cannot be remembered, a memory of something that cannot seem to be restored. The laws were created to try and clarify, purify, and perhaps encourage restoration.

DR: So, these were not in line with what Moses intended?

DS: We cannot agree to that statement. Even with Moses, there was a recognition of what was being lost and there was discussion on how to stop the loss, how to maintain connection to what were the beginnings. We will not say Moses was in complete agreement to all laws in Leviticus, but he saw the purpose of them. He thought they were worth the effort, because they did not know what they had lost, and did not know how to stop the loss. They blamed evolution; they blamed many things that were not to blame. But in their search to find a cause and heal the cause, many things were tried, and the laws were part of that reflection.

My viewpoint is from the Counsel as they witness the awareness grow that something is "lost". I can feel the Counsel's fascination at how evolution seems to dance over the Origins of Life memories and even more fascinating that the elders of the tribe could perceive this loss. It is another example of the evolution of awareness and consciousness taking place in the elders.

What also feels very important is that because the elders could feel this loss, they were attempting to create laws to restore what was lost and stop more from being lost. But here in the witness of the Counsel, I find there is no "peaceful prayer" space of guidance that I have witnessed before. Here I can see with the Counsel, that these are the minds of the elders coming together to try to "figure out" what to do. These laws do not feel the same as the "guidance" I witnessed with Moses and the others as they created the "commandments". When Moses and his group created those commandments, they used visions and consulted the memories of an elder.

In like a quick overview of these laws, I can see the elders coming together. I can perceive the discussions and the decisions from which these laws come into being. I find it fascinating that the very thing that is being lost is not reached for by these elders as they create the laws. I sense no prayer or connection, as there was in the journeys of Moses and the tribes. It is the experience of the elders only. <u>Amazing that the very thing they are trying to stop, these elders perpetuate by not seeking prayerful guidance.</u> I am not sensing or perceiving through the Counsel's witness, any attempt to "ask God" about these laws.

#9 Recording 1:07:51 *Priests vs Prophets*

DR: It seems there was contention between the prophets of the Bible and the old priesthood, the ones who did the animal sacrifices. Can you comment upon that antagonism?

DS: The Counsel likes your word "prophet". That is an appropriate word.

I see, through the Counsel's witness, that the prophets were those who still had moments of access to the gifts of Eden. They did not live in it; but they had moments of access, moments of clarity, moments of memory, moments of timelessness. But the priests did not have such. They were more of the mind, the thinking, the analysis, the rules. And there was some fear among the priests of those moments when the prophets were in the effect of the gifts of Eden. It was not comprehensible to the priests. And it feels as if it was the root of the antagonism, because what the prophets brought back with them had elements of such truth and holiness to it, that the priests could not discard it. But they could not explain it, and there was fear. Though it would not be recounted in your history as fear, we would suggest to you from our witness, that it was fear that was at the root of the antagonism between the priests and the prophets, because the prophets accessed, for moments of time, the gifts of Eden. And when they did, there was such truth and holiness about them that they could not be called anything but holy. And so, the priests were frustrated, aggravated is a good word, because they could not go there; and yet, they were holy men. They did not like it that the prophets could go where they could not go, and contention resulted.

There was a closedness in the minds of the priests that did not allow them to follow the prophets and their ways. They were too afraid. For the prophets to access the gifts of Eden, there was such faith and trust. And the priests were not quite capable of that same level. So again, there was more contention, more blame, more distrust, more frustration. The priests were attached to their definitions as holy men. They could not deny the holiness of the prophets, but they were frightened by the prophets simultaneously. It created such confusion and frustration. That is what gave birth to what you are calling the contention and aggravation.

As I travel with the Counsel to this time of priests and prophets, I can sense that there is a true and real difference between these two. Again, I can feel the Counsel's interest as this gap is created by the evolution of these two types of men. I can sense the Counsel's witness to the strength of the gifts of Eden in these "prophets" and I cannot hope but wonder if what channels like myself access now, is the same as what the prophets accessed back then. Could it be that the "gifts of Eden" are coming alive again in the art of channeling?

There was such contention between them and yet neither one was the enemy. I can sense that the priests, as frustrated as they are, cannot judge the prophets as wrong, for the holiness that they are is very obvious. I can feel the radiance from these prophets as I am viewing the whole scene from the Counsel's perspective. Their holiness is real and that truly fuels the aggravation the priests feel, for they cannot deny the holiness and the soundness of the wisdom the prophets speak.

#9 Recording 1:11:48 *Star of David Origin*

DR: The six-point Star of David, what is the origin of that, the symbol?

DS: It was brought back by a prophet, and the priests hoped that they would be able to use it to go where the prophets went. They had no understanding that their consciousness would not allow them. It could have been used this way and still can be, and in other generations has been used to ascend to, to move beyond the limited moment of your time. But the priests in their holy ways could not seem to access anything through it, and so it led to more frustration. But it was brought through by a prophet hoping to help the priests come to where he had been. But the consciousness of the priests would not open to allow the Star of David, the pointed star, to do what it could do on an energetic level. And so, it was a tool offered from a prophet to the priests, but there was no one among the priests that could be able to use it.

DR: Was it a power symbol, a gateway? How did the prophet use it?

DS: The prophet asked for a way to help others see as he saw, and was given this symbol that you now call the Star of David. It was a symbol that when put on the ground could, if one would surrender to it, transport awareness and consciousness. But the mind of the one who wants to use it must be faithful and open enough to allow their consciousness to be moved.

One or two of the priests attempted this. But when consciousness moves, there is a feeling that is unfamiliar, and they (the priests) thought was dangerous. So, they shut it down. And the prophet who brought it through was not thought to be helpful. They (the priests) took it to be a weapon, when it was not such. It was just that the movement of consciousness when one would sit within it, and follow its intention, would move the mind in ways that the priests had not ever moved before. And so great trust and faith is needed to follow the openings that are offered. To this day the symbol has power, but it is used in different ways by different ones. It doesn't have the same power now, that it had then, because it was empowered by the intention of the prophet who brought it in. We do not say it is powerless now, but like many things on your planet, it has evolved, and in its evolution it has become limited.

About how the prophet uses the Star of David, I am actually with the prophet in its use. I can sense the movement of consciousness. I can feel the openness of the prophet, and I can feel the need for that open trust that allows the Star of David to do what it can do when the prophet uses it. The feelings are very similar to what I experience when I open to channel. With channeling, as well, a degree of trust and faith is required. I find the similarities to how I channel quite fascinating.

Discussion

MOSES

#5 Recording 1:11:45 *Egyptians See Hebrews as Threat*

DS: As I perceive the story of the Egyptians, what made the Hebrews a threat was their refusal to evolve. And so, those that were evolving felt that the Hebrews were making them wrong. They weren't. The Hebrews just didn't want to go there. They were adhering to a simplicity. But in their simplicity, they were insulting those that weren't simple. And threatening them. Then on another level, they were poking the bear, in that the Hebrew's connection to the Origin of Life memory was stronger. And that activated the Egyptians' memory of the Origin of Life, and it started to disturb their slumber.

#5 **Recording 1:12:29** *Hebrews' Simple Life Creating Inequality*

DS: It's almost like an atheist sees a threat by someone with faith, because they don't want the question of God to be bothered. "No, I'm an atheist. Don't challenge me". And someone believing in God challenges them. No, it doesn't. "I just believe in God, and you don't". But it's like the question disturbs the atheist and makes those of faith challenging, and therefore, an enemy.

The inequality that came from the invention and the artisan was fascinating to see. To see curiosity and need invent, and then invention and artisan create an inequality, because person A did it and person D didn't. Person D was still farming wheat. Person A was molding gold. And it started the seeds of inequality.

And I could really see that the simplistic origins of life there were those who could, did, and those who couldn't, did something else. But in it all, there was an equality. And it was like the Hebrews were witnessing inequality coming out of invention, and so that made invention dangerous to them. They just wanted to stay simple. They wanted to stay away from it. That's where I would say the story of the golden idols and all the rest of it came from, because those of the simple belief saw the inequality that the artisanship and the invention was creating. There were those of the have and those of the have not. But the Hebrews never thought of themselves, those of the original life, as have not. They just lived simply. Anyway, it's fascinating.

#5 Recording 1:14:54 *Hebrews Escape*

DR: It's much bigger. The story of the pursuit of the Hebrews because they were escaped slaves turns out to be false. No, it wasn't because they were escaped slaves. It was because they threatened the emerging belief system. And then they (one Egyptian sect) wanted to extinguish them, not just recover and put them back.

DS: Oh no, and they were like a small section of Egypt that wanted the extinction. Not all of Egypt.

DR: Wow. And they escaped intact.

DS: They did.

DR: Did they escape in the middle of the night?

DS: Well, it took them a while to band together, which might be why you have all those stories of the plagues, and all of that time. There were all these separate families that were just living their hidden simple life, disturbing no one. And they kept getting more and more threatened. Then they started to band together, and realized that they couldn't stay in Egypt because they were being perceived as a threat. Moses sort of rallied them together, and then they left. And for the most part, they were allowed to leave except for this one sect, that's the best word, s-e-c-t. This one sect in Egypt said, "No, we can't let them leave. They are a threat to us. We have to extinguish them".

It was very similar to what happened in the Crusades when the Christians went back to Arabia and decided they had to

Christianize, and they wiped out those that wouldn't. It had the same feeling. Those that were chasing the Hebrews had the same feeling as the Crusades. Who sends soldiers to bring God's word? Not priests, but soldiers! Why are we sending soldiers to bring God's word? We sent soldiers to bring the word of God? No. You send priests; you don't send soldiers.

#5 Recording 1:17:32 *Moses' Parents*

DR: Did you get a sense of Moses being born to a Hebrew woman and raised as Egyptian. How does that resolve?

DS: Moses came from a marriage of love. I didn't say that earlier, but he came from a marriage of love. And his father loved his mother. And so made her his wife. The fact that she was Hebrew was hidden or overlooked.

DR: Oh, so an Egyptian married Moses' mother?

DS: His father was Egyptian; his mother was Hebrew.

DR: And was his father part of the ruling system, the court?

DS: They had influence; I won't say they were the top of the caste. He had enough influence to get away with marrying a Hebrew, and that was just hushed. Which I think is where the whole story of hiding the baby came from, because her background was hidden. It just wasn't spoken of.

DR: So that's resolved. Then he was raised as an Egyptian, and of some means.

DS: But his mother always taught him the old ways. Always. I could see him getting involved in Egyptian ways. And I could see him wearing gold. I could see his mother being concerned and calling him to task, and I could see him conflicting with her.

#5 Recording 1:18:58 *Moses' Memories Waken*

DS: But then he eventually returned to her (his mother) and said, "You're right". After the memories woke, that's when he went to his mother first, because his mother was the one who always held that for him.

DR: What was the retreat? Did he retreat someplace?

DS: That's what they did. The Hebrews, in order to maintain their simplicity, would just go away on retreats. There was conflict within him about something and he went on a retreat. And so that idea of the forty days is true. He was on a retreat when the memories opened.

DR: He went out to the desert. Is that when he met his father-in-law?

DS: I don't know. But he went on a retreat. I didn't see the father-in-law. What I saw was that he went on a retreat and on the retreat the memories opened. That makes sense to me, because in my own training over the last years, there's been various retreats and workshops I've gone on where I want to say memories have opened. And I understand things, and I know things, and I see things. And that's why I can do what I do now, because over the last thirty years I've been continually going on workshops and trainings and retreats. And each time I am able to access more. I am clearing away something.

DR: Did Moses confront the Pharaoh, the leadership?

DS: I didn't see that.

#5 Recording 1:22:20 *Red Sea Parting*

DR: The Counsel said they (the Counsel) impacted the supposed parting of the Red Sea.

DS: It was like they did something that made it (the effect of the parting) stronger.

DR: They put energy into it?

DS: Yes, there was already this movement of water in two different directions. Makes me think of a tidal bore where the water was going this way and that way from some storm or something. And because they'd been witnessing, they (the Counsel) decided to strengthen that, so that the Hebrews could actually walk on the ground across the sea. That's true.

DR: Did you see them walk on ground or just?

DS: I saw them walk on ground. Yes, they walked on ground.

#5 Recording 1:23:07 *Myth of Plagues*

DR: What's fascinating to me is that some of these stories have absolute basis in truth and others, like the plagues, have no basis in truth at all.

DS: Because the Hebrews were viewed as such a threat by the Egyptian sect, that wanted them to be extinguished, the Egyptian sect had to create a danger. And so, if there was a plague, then it could be blamed on the Hebrews. If there was a disease, if three Hebrews died, then it came from the Hebrews. It was a small sect, an extreme sect, and most of the Egyptians didn't agree with them, so they were trying to convince, and make a space for themselves (the Egyptian sect).

DR: But the Hebrews kept that myth of the plagues alive in the Passover story. They changed it around.

DS: You'll have to ask them (the Counsel) why. I don't know, but they do.

DR: They said these were plagues from God, put on the Egyptians, not from us. Wow! Talk about editing the story.

DS: But also, once the Hebrews reached Israel, they now were affected by the seeds of inequality. I mean judgment is rampant here (in our world) now. I don't think there's any religion that isn't affected by judgment. I don't know any human who isn't affected by judgment. And so it started in small places and eventually infected everything.

My sense, as I witnessed this, was the Hebrews were trying to stay out of being infected by that inequality, which is why they left.

#5 Recording 1:27:05 *Laws to Recreate the Old Ways*

DR: It's greed and selfishness that breeds desire and inequality.

DS: If you have wealth with the Origins of Life (respect, compassion, kindness), having what you need when you need it, then wealth doesn't corrupt you. But it's exactly what you're saying. And I think the laws, the commandments that Moses and the three of them put together, were made to re-institute living the old way.

#5 Recording 1:27:44 *Moses' Memories Opened*

DR: Did you see Moses go up to the mountain and come down?

DS: No. I didn't see him on a mountain. I saw him sitting in a meditative prayerful place. I felt lamentation within him; a cry to God to understand about the conflicts within him. The fight within himself between Egyptian and Hebrew. I saw him in lamentation, that's the only word I can use. And then that, that deep need opened up the memories, and what he called visions.

DR: On the retreat?

DS: On the retreat, yes.

DR: After the Hebrews escaped, did he talk to the whole group of tribes after they got out?

DS: Yes, he was definitely in charge of the tribes. He was in charge that whole time. And Moses lived a long time because of it. Because he was in charge of it, that almost kept him alive. So, he aged, but he was there through the whole time. But his memories didn't open in old age. I'm going to say he was forty when the memories opened. And the elder one was, the elder one of the three of them, was maybe fifty. And the younger was maybe twenty. Because I could see them sitting together and Moses sharing the vision, and then them trying to create laws that would help people to live that way. Thou shalt not covet thy neighbor's goods; thou shalt not covet thy neighbor's wife. Ways to live in the old way. How to support that and stay out of the selfishness. Fascinating.

#9 Recording1:30:05 *Star of David*

DR: When you saw the Star of David, the six-pointed star, and the prophet was showing a priest how to use it, and it has to be on the ground... they put it on the ground?

DS: Yes, he drew it and sat within it.

DR: He just drew it in the ground? It wasn't like a metal object?

DS: No, it was something he drew in the sand. And there was a true desire from the prophet to help the priests. The priests did not like being left behind the prophets. I don't know who the prophet was, but maybe it was a David. Is that why it was called David's star? I didn't see a name. It was just a prophet that with true loving intent wanting to help the priests be more like the prophets, so that the priests would understand the prophets. And two priests tried it and sat within it. I could feel as their consciousness started to shift, then the fear arose, and then they just stopped it. And so, they saw it as a weapon. They didn't see it as a tool.

CONCLUSION

My intent in starting this query was to see if I could get better information and answers to resolve some of the more perplexing questions surrounding the stories of the Hebrew Bible, specifically the Five Books of Moses.

We (Donna and I) received far more than we expected, not only getting wonderful answers that resolved most of the more perplexing questions we inquired about, but most importantly, getting messages of prime importance concerning the state of affairs of mankind. These messages fully explained the origin and evolution of some of the unfortunate behaviours of humans. Those behaviours apparently started with the exodus from Eden and the resulting necessity of hoarding of food for survival, a behaviour not needed within the confines of Eden. Over time, this hoarding "evolved or devolved" into worse patterns of behaviour towards one another including greed, selfishness, power-seeking, control over others, and worse.

These negative behaviours are sometimes blamed on temptations from a devil or similar 'evil' being. The channelings simply don't support this and instead clearly state that the devil or fallen angel concept is a human-created myth to explain how bad things happen.

From the channelings, we could blame the 'corrupting' interaction of the 'seeded' higher consciousness in Adam and Eve with the powerful evolutionary tendency on Earth for our negative behaviours but that is no better a solution than blaming a devil for our troubles. Taking a positive tack, solving this 'selfishness' issue is mankind's greatest challenge.

The messages of prime importance are that we, the humans, are fully responsible for our behaviour, that we are the ones that need to fix our many issues, and lastly, that there is going to be no intervention from above to save us. We are on our own.

Donna and I feel that we were successful in this effort to understand key events and people of the Hebrew Bible using a Q&A channeled approach. We obtained answers that we feel, in comparison to the stories of the Hebrew Bible, are more believable, more expansive of the events, and provide new insight into the feelings and psychology of the major figures of the Bible.

Every story that emerged from the channelings surprised me and greatly exceeded my expectations in every sense. Every story was different from what I could have predicted and, in all cases, either greatly enhanced the biblical version or presented the story and events in a much different way than it was written in the biblical account.

My belief before I started this investigation was that at least some of the more miraculous stories were simply made up, while others likely had some basis around an event. To me, being raised in the Jewish faith, I was amazed that the channelings verified that all of the people and events asked about actually happened, albeit not necessarily in the way written in the Hebrew Bible. I would not have believed in advance that this was the case. Rather I would have thought that some stories were embellished while other were completely made up. It is a testament to those who recorded, preserved, and passed on the stories through the generations that there is still strong truth in the writings.

One example of a story that is hard to believe is the story of Noah and the Flood. How could one man and his family build a huge boat and rescue two or more of every creature on Earth? This is not to likely to be believed by rational humans. But if the channelings are correct, there was catastrophic flooding with major loss of life, but it was not a global event with the entire world under water. And even though there was not an actual person named Noah, there were several people who fit that bill; had warnings, built ships, rescued their families, and even rescued animals trying to escape the rising waters. Noah was a composite, and the flooding was not an act of God. Still, the event occurred with its calamitous impact on the Earth, its fauna and flora, and changed the beliefs of the surviving humans.

Given the nature of human beings, it is not surprising that many of the stories were embellished and changed from the original, given the lengthy time period from the occurrence until the story was set down in words. There were also indications in the channelings that some events, such as the

Flood, which were ascribed to be acts of God, were written that way deliberately. In that time period, this actually strengthened beliefs, since they described a God watching over humankind and rewarding or punishing good or bad behaviour respectively. In today's world, with much greater understanding of causality of natural events, most would dismiss this kind of idea of reward/punishment by an angry God. But in previous eras, the impact of such stories of an angry God or a saviour God seems to have had a beneficial effect on the populace in terms of strengthening belief in God and in moral behaviour.

It was not my intention in this query to ask about major societal issues such as science versus religion or creation versus evolution. My original interest was simply to ask about the major characters of the Hebrew Bible from Genesis to Deuteronomy. However, the answers to my questions actually resolved, at least in my mind, some of these ongoing issues, especially between science and religion. In the channelings, there is no dispute between the two. Creation and evolution work hand in hand in the creation of humans of higher consciousness (Adam and Eve) with evolutionary forces leading to the subsequent growth of mankind. These subsequent changes appear to have been about ways of thinking and understanding as well as technological advancements due to the evolutionary driving forces acting upon these new humans.

Even though the stories from our channelings differ from the Biblical stories, there is still a core that is consistent between the two. In the comparison, there are just far more explanations and details in the channeled version.

The Biblical statement of the creation of Adam says that he

was created literally from the Earth, *"The LORD God formed man from the dust of the earth."* (Genesis 2:7)

The channeling says the same thing, but with more elaboration and explanation. "The body was created from elements, and we use the word elements in a chemical way, elements from the Earth itself. It was important that this body was of the Earth and not of us. It was important that it would fit in with the Earth, would need what the Earth has, would breathe what the Earth breathes, and would live as the Earth lives. And so, its chemicals, its chemistry came from the Earth elements. (Section 1, Discussion: Adam & Eve **#4 Recording 1:00:56** *Creating Adam and Eve, page 118*).

The channeling describes a scientific approach to the creation, and explains why it was important to use Earth elements. From a biological point of view, the new humans needed to be harmonious with the Earth, perhaps analogous to blood type compatibility in transfusions.

The Biblical phrase describing Adam coming to life is *"He blew into his nostrils the breath of life, and man became a living being."* (Genesis 2:7).

The analogous portion of the channeling is "I see that the creation came to life when the soul occupied it. I can see that what the chemistry created did not come to life until the soul occupied it."

"And the Counsel says the creation body of Adam did not come to life until the soul occupied it". That is our (the Counsel) belief, which was how we create." (Section 1, Chapter 1, Creating Adam & Eve, **#3 Recording 18:20** *Creation Process, page 47*).

So again, there is consistency between the two with the former from the Bible, perhaps, being more poetic. Both passages describe a body being created first and then coming to life after a "life-force" inhabits the body. Chemistry alone did not create a living being, both creation and science were part of the process.

The Biblical statement of Eve being fashioned from part of Adam is, *"He took one of his ribs and closed up the flesh at that spot. And the Lord God fashioned the rib that he had taken from the man into a woman."* (Genesis 2:21-22).

This is hard to accept, that God would need to cut open Adam and take a rib. Why not just create a second human in the same manner as the first? And did Adam ever get his rib back or did it grow back?

In the channeling, the explanation of this creation is "The myth of the rib of Adam feels to be more because the cells of the marrow in the bone were part of the basic recipe of the second body. (Section 1, Chapter 1, Creating Adam & Eve **#2 Recording 17:51** *Pair Created with Distinct Differences, page 42*).

This is a far better explanation and one that directly links creation with science. It was not the whole rib that was taken, but marrow bone cells which retain the ability to become any type of cell. Therefore, these cells theoretically can be used to make an entire human body. It would seem reasonable to assume that at the time this story was passed on, orally and then written, that humans would not have had the scientific understanding of cells and tissue culture; therefore, the explanation given in the Bible of using a rib is perfectly understandable.

As a scientist and geneticist, I was very interested in getting more scientific details of the creation of Adam and Eve, especially after learning about the use of Earth materials in the creation. It wasn't until a post-recording discussion that Donna recalled a vision she had had of an actual facility in which the construction of the bodies took place.

"DR: Do you get a sense at all with Adam and Eve, that they were constructed on the planet? Was there some kind of place, building?

DS: It was a silver. I want to say steel, like a silver room. There was glass. And first there was Adam. And there was a pillar of light that came out of the ceiling. There was... a tube, a big tube coming out of the ceiling, maybe 18 inches in diameter. And there was two or three of them in the ceiling. And the first one, that's where Adam was. And the energy came out of that, and it connected to a small tube on the bottom. And that's where Adam was created.

And interesting, when they created Eve, Eve was in the tube next to him. And when I was watching it, it was like Adam wasn't completely finished when they decided to create Eve. So, he was still in the tube. He wasn't a walking, talking being. He was still in the tube. But he was formed." (Section 1, Discussion: Adam & Eve **#4 Recording 1:00:56** *Creating Adam & Eve, page 118*).

This passage was extraordinarily thrilling for me to hear – advanced beings used a laboratory to construct human bodies, and that they weren't just created by waving a magic wand!

So again, the channeling clearly indicates that Creation is

using scientific methodology in the creation of Adam and Eve. Creation is the driving force behind the Adam and Eve creation.

Although the Bible says simply that "*The Lord God formed man*" (Genesis 2:7), the channelings indicate that other entities, working at different levels, were involved in the creating process.

"So, the Counsel believes they are creating. But in actuality CREATION is using the Counsel to experiment in creating. So, there are two levels to what we are seeing as it is presented to you." (Section 1, Chapter 1 **#2 Recording 9:36** *Creating of Adam & Eve on Earth, page 40*).

According to the channelings, there were several levels of beings or entities involved in this creation. It appears that a counsel of beings is directly involved in the physical process whereas a higher level, CREATION–Creator–God, is influencing or causing this event to happen. *To paraphrase a current expression, this is way beyond my pay grade of understanding.* I just ask questions....

The Bible states that Adam and Eve were the first humans. This is difficult to reconcile with the archaeological evidence of primitive humans existing for at least a few million years since Adam and Eve were not primitive humanoids.

This is resolved in the channeling which describes the importance of the Adam and Eve creation.

"DR: So was this the first time this had been done where a life force at that level was brought to Earth and then put into a human body? Was that the experiment then? Was this the first time that this had been done successfully?

DS: The first time successfully on the Earth…" (Section 1, Chapter 1 **#2 Recording 9:36** *Creating of Adam & Eve on Earth, page 40).*

This was a unique event, not the first humanoids on the planet but the first 'conscious' human beings, created with a higher consciousness than that of the existing humanoids.

The channelings also resolved the issue of differing opinions about the purpose of sex, with some holding that it is solely for procreation and nothing more than that.

"But we wanted some uniqueness to it. And we were dealing with the loneliness of the Adam. There was a recognition in the loneliness of Adam entering form, that we wanted to allow, we wondered if we could allow relationship. If we could make the procreation a method, if it could be less animalistic and more something else…

We wanted consciousness connected to the instinctive procreation. Because that was the purpose, to introduce a consciousness. And so, we wanted the consciousness to differentiate the humans from the animals and we wanted consciousness involved in procreation." (Section 1, Chapter 1, **#3 Recording 27:17** *Differences Between Adam & Eve, page 53).*

"DR: Yes, so this was more of wanting to see if they could create a bond, a feeling that was different from just animal coupling?

DS: Yes, we had witnessed it in some of your creatures. But the consciousness that we intended to place on the Earth was much more evolved than the care of a mother lion for her cub. And so, we simply connected, *the only word I can use*, the consciousness to the instincts of procreation and the instincts of natural protection, preservation, to the consciousness. When we simply made the connection, we didn't design what that would do. We simply made the connection like you would connect the wires, and then let the engines run." (Section 1, Chapter 1, **#3 Recording 27:17** *Differences Between Adam & Eve*).

So, the creation of Adam and Eve not only included the ability to procreate but also included something more, a bonding and relationship forming ability as part of sex. From this perspective, it is a mistake to insist that the sex act is solely for procreation. It was not intended that way.

In summary, higher consciousness was brought to Earth via Adam and Eve to enhance the evolution of humans that were beginning to show signs of more advanced thinking. Much of that higher consciousness that started at Eden was lost in subsequent generations. Both Abraham and Moses were able to recall the memories of Eden and re-invigorate the Hebrews with that way of life, which was one of simplicity, honesty, and cooperativeness. That life in Eden needed no rules of behaviour, because the higher consciousness that was brought to Earth in the Adam and the Eve knew innately how to behave and how to treat others.

The guidance given by the Counsel, unasked but critical, would be that returning to the way of life begun in Eden would seem to be human's greatest challenge, and what is most needed for the benefit of all humans on this planet.

Dan

✻✳✳

And from this space of **WE**, we offer this new understanding of old information. Here, we offer an understanding of how we did this. Our hope is that it serves you. That it raises questions in your mind and loosens your hold on what you think you can and cannot do. That it opens your mind to new ideas and exploration through the questions we have raised for you with this book. This book is not offered as new biblical truths, but rather to say what are biblical truths.

As spoken in Chapter 0, this book, like the Bible, is offered as roadmap to simple understandings as a method to see our own personal self in terms of who we are becoming. To make each of us aware that we are still evolving. That EVOLUTION is still at work with us each, individually; to ask if we are in fact cooperating with EVOLUTION or working against it. Are we now driven by what we know and what we want? Or by what is possible and what we can become?

We offer this new perspective of the simple truths that began in Eden, to awaken an idea that they can still have a place in our world today. For these simple truths to be found in our world today, they must first find their way into our individual lives. That can happen when we return to the simplicity of caring for one another, neighbours or family; of supporting one another, friends, or foes; of believing in each other through the release of blaming, dominance, and "me" first.

It is my fervent hope that we have challenged your thinking with the facts as the Counsel has relayed them here; that we have touched your heart by making the faith and trust of such men as Abraham and Moses much more real; and, that we have left you with food for thought about how CREATION and EVOLUTION do in fact work together and not separately, one against the other.

If I can be this what else can I be? EVOLUTION, CREATION…allow them to become more real and see where they can take you, where they can take our world. Let's continue to evolve and grow. Let go of the feeling of being a finished product and move beyond what we know and what we have become comfortable with. Let this book make you uncomfortable and see what you can find in your discomfort. This is what we did here.

Amen.

Donna and the Counsel

ACKNOWLEDGMENTS

From Dan Ronis

This book is dedicated to my mother Geraldine Ronis (nee Zendel) a teacher, a feminist, a shy spiritual woman who loved learning above all else and who encouraged me from above.

I am grateful for the four women who helped birth this book: Donna Somerville, my co-author, who generously donated her time and talent, to Patricia Dale who for her insight and guiding words, to my editor, Fay Thompson, who artfully crafted the book into its final form with a woman's touch, and to Kelsey Pavier whose artwork graces the cover.

To the women who unknowingly helped inspire this book by living lives of strength, integrity, and faith, Esther Turner (Washington D.C.) and sisters Beryl and Karen Stovell (Ontario, Canada).

Lastly, my life has been greatly enriched these last fourteen years thanks to my wife and partner, Nancy A. Lease.

From Donna Somerville

When I considered acknowledgements for my part in this book, they are first to those people who demonstrated what could be accessed through "channeling" and how they generously taught and encouraged me in that direction. Of course, next is my husband, David Somerville, who has stood by me and supported me since 1988, through an interesting and varied journey of life. We met in a meditation class and began exploring from that point until now. Our journey of discovery continues.

Specifically, I want to name those that demonstrated what channeling could be. First, now passed away, Barbara Eagles (Ontario, Canada) who scared me with what she could access and bring through. And then, Frank Alper (Arizona, USA), also passed away, who demonstrated the next level of channel. And then finally, multiple teachers who generously encouraged me in a direction I explored with trepidation and uncertainty of which my most influential was Bonnie Bielous (Minnesota, USA). Thank you to them all.

Thank you to the many clients, who over these years, have trusted me to open and see for them, thereby stretching me in new directions. My practice with them has led me to what I was able to bring through for this book.

To Dan, who asked, "could you answer some questions" and trusted me to do so. Thank you.

And finally, to my inner self who has so bravely travelled "the road less travelled" and done so with grace and wonderful faith. And, of course, to the souls of these interesting women of the Hebrew Bible, who have opened themselves to me, so that we could explore and understand the lives they lived and how they lived them. Thank you.

BIBLIOGRAPHY

The Torah: The Five Books of Moses. (1962). The Jewish Publication Society of America.

Gunther Plaut, W. G.(ed.) (2005). General Introduction to the Torah. In: The Torah: A Modern Commentary. UJR Press

de Lange, N. (1992). Atlas of the Jewish World. Andromeda (Oxford) Ltd.

INSPIRATIONAL AUTHORS
ON DAN'S BOOKSHELF:

Richard E. Friedman – <u>Who Wrote the Bible?</u>

Jane Roberts - <u>Seth Speaks</u> and other titles by Roberts

Michael Newton – <u>Journey of Souls, Destiny of Souls, Memories of the Afterlife</u>

Phyllis V. Schlemmer – <u>The Only Planet of Choice</u>

Andrew Ramer – <u>Revelations for a New Millenium</u>

Thaddeus Golas - <u>The Lazy Man's Guide to Enlightenment</u>

Stephen Gaskin - <u>Monday Night Class</u>

Glenn Kittler – <u>Edgar Cayce on the Dead Sea Scrolls</u>

Lytle Robinson – <u>Edgar Cayce's Story of The Origin and Destiny of Man</u>

INSPIRATIONAL AUTHORS ON DONNA'S BOOKSHELF:

Paul Ferrini – <u>Love Without Conditions, Reflections of the Christ Mind</u>

Helen Schucman and William Thetford – <u>A Course In Miracles</u>

Richard Bach – <u>Illusions – The Adventures of a Reluctant Messiah</u>

Eckhart Tolle – <u>Power of Now</u>

Don Miguel Ruiz with Janet Mills – <u>The Voice of Knowledge</u>

Joe Dispenza – <u>Breaking the Habit of Being Yourself</u>

Michael Singer – <u>The Untethered Soul</u>

ABOUT THE AUTHORS

DANIEL H. RONIS is a retired scientist whose lifelong interest in religions and spiritual knowledge has led to the creation of this book. He is continuing this lifelong adventure taking courses in religious studies at a local university as part of a certificate in Jewish-Christian origins. He is hopeful that this effort will continue with one or more additional books on topics of personal interest.

DONNA SOMERVILLE is not an author, but a channel. One who has learned and then practised the art of opening to another place in space and time, to bring through wisdoms and perspectives to help change how we view the lives we live and how we live them. Donna has been doing this channeling work full time since 1994. The use of channel in creating this book took her work in a new direction. Donna had worked with other authors, but in a very arms length approach. These channelings with Dan are much more involved and much more intriguing; a real step away from the one on one, personal channelings Donna has been doing for so long.